HOCKEY'S *Most Amazing* RECORDS

Transcontinental Books
1100 René-Lévesque Boulevard West
24th floor
Montreal (Quebec) H3B 4X9
Tel.: 514 340-3587
Toll-free 1-866-800-2500
www.livres.transcontinental.ca

**Bibliothèque et Archives nationales du Québec and Library and Archives
Canada cataloguing in publication**

Main entry under title:
Hockey's Most Amazing Records
At head of title: The Hockey News.

ISBN 978-0-9813938-7-2

1. Hockey - Records - North America. 2. National Hockey League - Miscellanea.
I. Fraser Edward, 1978- . II. The Hockey News (Montréal, Québec).

GV847.5.N44 2011   796.962'6409   C2011-941503-8

Proofreading: Ronnie Shuker
Photo editor: Erika Vanderveer
Layout: Diane Marquette
Page design: Annick Désormeaux and Anne-Laure Jean
Cover design: Jamie Hodgson

Printed in Canada
© Transcontinental Books, 2011
Legal deposit – 3rd quarter 2011
National Library of Quebec
National Library of Canada

We acknowledge the financial support of the Government of Canada through the Canada
Book Fund for our publishing activities and the Government of Quebec through the SODEC
Tax Credit for our publishing activities.

For information on special rates for corporate libraries and wholesale purchases,
please call 1-866-800-2500.

The Hockey News

Edited by Edward Fraser

HOCKEY'S *Most Amazing* RECORDS

Transcontinental Books

For Sloane, Mom and Dad.

TABLE OF CONTENTS

TABLE OF CONTENTS

Big, Bad & Steely

Top Of The Flops

Working Overtime

Chasing Stan

TABLE OF CONTENTS

Bruin something special

Soft Pads, Soft Hands

Tough Stuff

Fare game

TABLE OF CONTENTS

And Howe!

They Call it a Streak

Shooting Gallery

Travels & Travails

First & Foremost

TABLE OF CONTENTS

That's a Stretch

Red Light District

INTRODUCTION

I t's the highest notch on the stick against which we measure greatness. The pursuit to topple a standard keeps us riveted and when it does fall we almost immediately shift focus to the next pursuer in a never-ending race. Captivating. Awe-inspiring. Rarefied.

The record.

It's a concept that piques the interest of those on both sides of the glass. To be the very best in any regard is something special – a theme you'll see again and again on following pages. "Special" certainly refers to the talent needed to reach unparalleled heights, but it also emerges in the form of cherished memories. NHLers past and present treat the spotlight as though it burns, but most can't resist a detailed recollection and an admission that their feat holds a unique place in their heart.

And therein lies the inspiration for this project. Each record, no matter how significant, has a story worth sharing.

We begin with a closer look at Wayne Gretzky, Martin Brodeur and the Montreal Canadiens, all three synonymous with their statistical accomplishments. They, of course, are known for their grandeur; of the 104 official NHL records they hold between them, not one pockmarks their legends.

That isn't, however, always the case with the subsequent 125 amazing records. Most are moments worthy of pride, but included amongst our favorites are the undesired, the unintended, the comedic.

A touch of sour with the sweet, but unforgettable nonetheless. From consecutive Cups to cups of coffee; from soft hands to bloody paws; from bright lights to red lights. After months of research and probably-more-than-necessary heated debates within THN-HQ, we've whittled down thousands of various NHL records into what I believe is an engrossing, entertaining mix. I hope you will as well.

EDWARD FRASER
MANAGING EDITOR
THE HOCKEY NEWS

The Record-Breakers

WAYNE GRETZKY

He didn't break records. He vaporized them.

Wayne Gretzky has been gone for 12 seasons and has lost exactly two of the 61 NHL regular season, playoff and All-Star Game records with which he retired: regular season overtime assists and All-Star Game assists.

But in the ultimate manifestation of his endurance as the greatest player who ever will live, Gretzky gained a record, and a big one, since he quit. During Mario Lemieux's comeback from 2000 to 2006, the 2.05 points-per-game average with which he initially retired in 1997 dropped to 1.88, putting it below Gretzky's 1.92.

"Didn't know that," Gretzky said.

A surprising admission considering The Great One's depth of knowledge. Extremely few of his artifacts at the Hall of Fame or his childhood home in Brantford, Ont., are not cataloged in his brain.

During his career there were some individual game marks that, of course, they had to tell him about after the buzzer, but otherwise he hunted down every single-season and career statistical milestone with unwavering ambition, fully aware of the chase.

"To be quite honest, I loved them all," Gretzky said of his records. "But 50 (goals) in 39 (games) is probably my favorite because it will be the hardest to break."

This is from the same guy who told teammate Kevin Lowe the morning of the day he scored five times against the Flyers to hit 50 during that 1981-82 season that one more game might be all he needed. Point is, he drove himself to do it all, then was delighted to learn there still was something remaining.

So many records, so few millenniums remaining for someone to break them. Now that another generation has failed to approach any of Gretzky's biggies, presumably the task is left for extraterrestrials. The NHL remains an equal opportunity employer, so one never knows. Until 'The Next One' climbs out of a saucer threading saucer passes, it is as safe as Dave

Wayne Gretzky

Semenko kept Gretzky to assume his regular season career point record will fall when mountains do.

"Not as long as they still are playing 5-on-5," said Hall of Famer Bob Clarke, the gold standard of playmakers until Gretzky's arrival. "And with a league this big, I don't think any team is going to dominate in the playoffs to the point where anybody will play enough games to approach what he did there, either."

Gretzky, who has more assists (1,963) than Mark Messier, the No. 2 all-time scorer with 1,887, has points, played 14 years after the last of his four 200-plus point seasons – the only four in history – and never did better than 183 points. The decline was a reflection of the NHL's evolution into the Dead Puck Era then to the shot-block-a-thon it has become today.

Gretzky always maintained one should be judged only against his contemporaries. Clarke believes that's exactly the point.

"Gretzky playing today would be a long ways down from those totals of his biggest years," Clarke said. "But the second-best guy still would be a long ways down from him.

"I think it's a fairly decent gap down from Gretzky to, in my opinion, the second-greatest player in the game's history, Bobby Orr. We were able to stop Orr in the 1974 final. Well, not stop him, but we could live with him, control him somewhat. Nobody could control Gretzky.

"The brilliance from behind the net was one thing we had never seen at that level. But for me, his real innovation was how he would enter the zone, pull up, wait and hit somebody coming late in full stride.

"When I came into the league, Stan Mikita was the standard for seeing the ice and I thought he was brilliant. Bryan Trottier had tremendous vision, but didn't rely on it. He was more of a bull, creating room for (Mike) Bossy as much with that as with passing.

"The only one who resembled Gretzky would have been Lemieux. He had great vision, but I don't think was nearly as competitive. He complained, even threatened to drop out. Gretzky just played the game the way it was on the ice, never once complained.

"He played so well and so hard and never asked for a break. Lemieux asked for breaks. I never saw the love for the game in Lemieux that I saw in Gretzky."

For the record, Gretzky thought Clarke, remembered mostly for his will and tactics, set the vision standard.

"I studied how he ran power plays out of corners," Gretzky said. "Bobby took playmaking to another level, especially from the corners and from behind the net, something he never got enough credit for doing.

And for the curls inside the blueline?

"I watched how Gilbert Perreault would wait and hit the late guy," Gretzky said.

One star studies and improves on the next, the natural evolution of the game. But 163 assists in one season when nobody else has ever had more than 114 – and Gretzky beat that latter total seven times – didn't elevate a game so much as blow it up and start it over again to a degree practiced by only three athletes in history.

> ## "50 (goals) in 39 (games) is probably my favorite because it will be the hardest to break."
> ### Wayne Gretzky

Babe Ruth, with the help of a new, juiced-up ball, raised Gavvy Cravath's home run record of 24 to 54, 59 then 60. When Ruth hit 59 in 1921, Ken Williams of the St. Louis Browns was second with 24. Wilt Chamberlain raised Bob Pettit's NBA record of 29.24 points-per-game season average to 50.36 within three years. And Gretzky took Phil Esposito's goal record from 76 to 92 and his points record from 145 to 215.

Gordie Howe played 1,767 NHL games, during which he scored 801 goals. Gretzky beat that record by 650 games, getting No. 802 in his 1,117th contest. It took Howe 26 seasons to score 1,850 points. Gretzky topped that mark – at the end by 1,007 – in nearly 300 fewer games and is ahead of Mark Messier, who ascended to No. 2 on the all-time list, by 970. Gretzky's career total of 1,963 assists is 714 more than No. 2 on the list, Ron Francis.

Steve Hirdt of the Elias Sports Bureau once computed that scoring 970 more points than Howe – No. 2 on the list at the time – was similar in percentage terms to a baseball player hitting 1,166 career home runs, 404 more than leader Barry Bonds. And having 861 more assists than No. 2 Paul Coffey was equivalent to a player breaking Pete Rose's career hit record of 4,256 with 7,581, an increase of 3,325. That's how much better Gretzky was than anybody at that point.

"I don't know what numbers I would get now," Gretzky said. "These players are tremendous athletes and there are more of them with greater mobility than when I played. And the goaltending equipment is lighter and bigger, too.

"I always said it was really hard to compare eras; I'm not just saying that now. It is harder to score now in a lot of ways. And as committed as these guys now are to conditioning, I don't think we will see guys playing 24 or 25 years like Messier and (Chris) Chelios. Players are making enough money that I don't think they are going to want to.

"The only thing I will say is that there is less clutching and grabbing and more power plays per game on average. So, sure, my records could be broken. Nobody thought somebody would come along like Bobby Orr and nobody thought anybody would be productive as long as was Gordie.

"I think it's a fairly decent gap down from Gretzky to, in my opinion, the second-greatest player in the game's history, Bobby Orr."
Bobby Clarke

"You would have to be fortunate to play on a good team and you have to stay healthy."

Sidney Crosby and Alex Ovechkin, the two most dynamic players in today's game, have one scoring title each thus far, both won by six points. Pretty exciting stuff – if you were blissfully unaware of the hockey from three decades ago.

It was a time before the Dead Puck Era, with its obsessive defensive coaching, big butterflying goalies and protective equipment that encouraged so much more shot-blocking. There was room to move and access to the net, but enforcement being much more lax in Gretzky's time, his points came at a price, too.

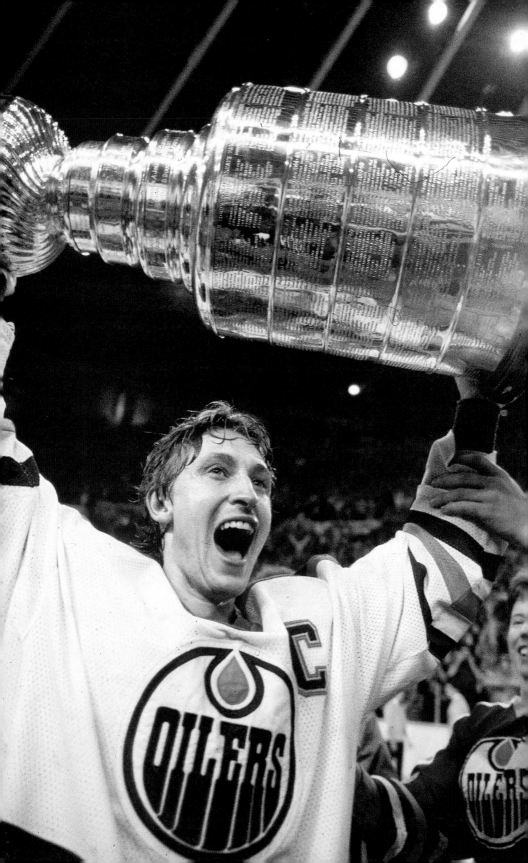

"That was part of the game," he said. "Before we played the Islanders, I knew (Isles coach) Al Arbour was talking about running me because I heard (Oilers coach) Glen Sather say the same thing about (Mike) Bossy."

However, he has no complaints.

"I used to cherish going into Boston Garden and the Spectrum, competing against Jean Ratelle and Bob Clarke," Gretzky continued. "They played hard, they didn't complain. You did the best you could with the situation. For me, the greatest thing in the world was to play in the NHL. If you didn't like it, go find another job.

"For me, the greatest thing in the world was to play in the NHL."
Wayne Gretzky

"I truly loved (chasing records). The two times I felt pressure the most was No. 76, when Phil was following me around city to city and I felt bad he had to do that. And 50 goals in 39, I knew it was special and obviously I was on a time limit."

Thanks to Gretzky, there is no such hurry anymore. While we wait patiently for challengers to the NHL's most coveted records, we can only rely on video and recollections. And, again, guess whose memory is far better than anybody else's.

"I cherished every record and I remember almost everything, really," Gretzky said. "If I run into somebody I played against as an 11-year-old, I can tell them in what game, what tournament. I remember every game at the Madison Square Garden, every one at Maple Leaf Gardens.

"I can't remember to comb my hair in the morning. But I remember everything else." ▌ Jay Greenberg

◄ After losing to the Islanders in back-to-back finals, Wayne Gretzky finally got his hands on the Cup in 1984.

WAYNE GRETZKY
OFFICIAL NHL RECORDS

GOALS: **894**

GOALS, INCLUDING PLAYOFFS: **1,016**

GOALS, ONE SEASON: **92, 1981-82 (80 GP)**

GOALS, ONE SEASON, INCLUDING PLAYOFFS: **100, 1983-84 (87; 13)**

GOALS, 50 GAMES FROM START OF SEASON: **61, 1981-82, 1983-84**

GOALS, ONE PERIOD: **4, Feb. 18, 1981 vs. St. Louis (3rd period)***

ASSISTS: **1,963**

ASSISTS, INCLUDING PLAYOFFS: **2,223**

ASSISTS, ONE SEASON: **163, 1985-86 (80 GP)**

ASSISTS, ONE SEASON, INCLUDING PLAYOFFS: **174, 1985-86 (163; 11)**

ASSISTS, ONE GAME: **7, three times***

ASSISTS, ONE ROAD GAME: **7, Dec. 11, 1985 vs. Chicago***

POINTS: **2,857**

POINTS, INCLUDING PLAYOFFS: **3,239**

POINTS, ONE SEASON: **215, 1985-86 (80 GP)**

POINTS, ONE SEASON, INCLUDING PLAYOFFS: **255, 1984-85 (208; 47)**

GOALS BY A CENTER: **894**

GOALS BY A CENTER, ONE SEASON: **92, 1981-82 (80 GP)**

ASSISTS BY A CENTER, CAREER: **1,963**

ASSISTS BY A CENTER, ONE SEASON: **163, 1985-86 (80 GP)**

POINTS BY A CENTER, CAREER: **2,857**

POINTS BY A CENTER, ONE SEASON: **215, 1985-86 (80 GP)**

ASSISTS BY A PLAYER IN HIS FIRST NHL SEASON, ONE GAME: **7, Feb. 15, 1980 vs. Washington**

HIGHEST GOALS-PER-GAME AVERAGE, ONE SEASON (MIN. 50 GOALS): **1.18, 1983-84**

HIGHEST ASSISTS-PER-GAME AVERAGE, CAREER (MIN. 300 ASSISTS): **1.32**

HIGHEST ASSISTS-PER-GAME AVERAGE, ONE SEASON (MIN. 35 ASSISTS): **2.04, 1985-86**

HIGHEST POINTS-PER-GAME AVERAGE, CAREER (MIN. 500 POINTS): **1.921**

HIGHEST POINTS-PER-GAME AVERAGE, ONE SEASON (MIN. 50 POINTS): **2.77, 1983-84**

40-OR-MORE GOAL SEASONS: **12**

CONSECUTIVE 40-OR-MORE GOAL SEASONS: **12, 1979-1991**

50-OR-MORE GOAL SEASONS: **9***

60-OR-MORE GOAL SEASONS: **5***

CONSECUTIVE 60-OR-MORE GOAL SEASONS: **4, 1981-1985**

100-OR-MORE POINT SEASONS: **15**

CONSECUTIVE 100-OR-MORE POINT SEASONS: **13, 1979-1992**

THREE-OR-MORE GOAL GAMES, CAREER: **50**

THREE-OR-MORE GOAL GAMES, ONE SEASON: **10, 1981-82, 1983-84**

CONSECUTIVE GAMES WITH AN ASSIST: **23, 1990-91**

CONSECUTIVE GAMES WITH A POINT: **51, 1983-84**

CONSECUTIVE GAMES WITH A POINT FROM START OF SEASON: **51, 1983-84**

GOALS IN PLAYOFFS: **122**

ASSISTS IN PLAYOFFS: **260**

ASSISTS, ONE PLAYOFF YEAR: **31, 1988**

ASSISTS IN ONE SERIES (OTHER THAN FINAL): **14, 1985 vs. Chicago***

ASSISTS IN FINAL SERIES: **10, 1988 vs. Boston**

ASSISTS, ONE PLAYOFF GAME: **6, April 19, 1987 vs. Los Angeles***

ASSISTS, ONE PLAYOFF PERIOD: **3, five times***

POINTS IN PLAYOFFS: **382**

POINTS, ONE PLAYOFF YEAR: **47, 1985**

POINTS IN FINAL SERIES: **13, 1988**

POINTS, ONE PLAYOFF PERIOD: **4, April 12, 1987 vs. Los Angeles***

SHORTHAND GOALS, ONE PLAYOFF YEAR: **3, 1983***

SHORTHAND GOALS, ONE PLAYOFF GAME: **2, April 6, 1983, April 25, 1985***

GAME-WINNING GOALS IN PLAYOFFS, CAREER: **24***

THREE-OR-MORE-GOAL GAMES IN PLAYOFFS, CAREER: **10**

*TIED

MARTIN BRODEUR

T welve Angry Shooters, sequestered with the task of convicting the greatest thief in hockey history, would need special instructions from the judge to cover all counts of the indictment.

"If the question was the playoffs, there would be a hung jury," said Glenn 'Chico' Resch, who, after 14 years as an NHL goalie and 15 seasons as the Devils' television analyst, does not have to steal anybody else's opinion. "But if Marty Brodeur is going to be charged with goal robbery, the verdict would come back unanimously guilty as the greatest regular season goalie of all-time."

Indeed, the NHL's all-time leader in regular season victories (625), shutouts (116) and 40-win seasons (eight, a staggering five more than anybody else) has so much loot stashed that he needs three different hideouts.

"I have a nice little bar at home that has a lot of nice stuff," Brodeur said. "The trainers keep some and my dad keeps some. I have kids and the family is really into it.

"Since I've started, I've kept all my stuff. I have sticks and pads from when I won Stanley Cups and every time I'm going to break a record I play with a different jersey. The shutout record I only played with one because I didn't know when I was going to get it, but for the win record I was wearing four (warmup and three periods) each game.

"I have the net for (record win) No. 552 at home. I cut little pieces every now and then so people can raise money for charities. It's such a big net, it's kind of cool I can help so many people."

It's going to be practically impossible for anyone to replicate the success Brodeur has had. At 39, his 1,132 games are 460 in front of the only remotely logical current challenger, Roberto Luongo, who is 32. If Brodeur never plays another game – and he plans to go at least through 2011-12 – Luongo, who has 308 wins, will need eight more 40-victory seasons to pass Brodeur's victory total and 61 shutouts to beat the bagel mark.

"It's like (Wayne Gretzky's) 92 goals (in a season)," Resch said. "How is anybody going to beat it?"

Only three goalies – Carey Price, Cam Ward and Miikka Kiprusoff – played 70 or more games in 2010-11. Ward and Price did it for the first time. Kiprusoff, who will turn 35 early in 2011-12, has done it in six seasons and he still is six short of Brodeur.

Catching him will be an assignment ever taller than the weeds in the New Jersey swamp where Brodeur has played most of his career for a team determined to call no attention to itself while routinely winning games by a scoreline of 3-1 or 2-0.

Brodeur has performed under the perfect conditions to rack up wins, but he also did a great job of adapting to that environment. And Brodeur's unique stand-up style has served him extremely well, saving his knees and hips from the taxing wear and tear that can come from the butterfly style most goalies employ now.

"He was the greatest first-save goalie in the NHL and of course he stopped some crucial rebounds, too," Resch said. "But at the back of a well-constructed team protecting its goalie, he could stand up on his angles and make stops without having to butterfly, which never has been his game."

Prior to 2005-06, when the NHL implemented the trapezoid that limits where goalies can play the puck, Brodeur also did himself and his defensemen a huge favor by being a fantastic puckhandler, which allowed him to prevent many dump-ins from ever becoming scoring chances.

And while Brodeur's style and ability to play the puck preserved physical fatigue, his between-the-ears approach also did wonders for relieving stress, too.

"You can see the energy Ryan Miller expends getting ready for a game," Resch said. "Marty and (Dominik) Hasek were in the locker room staying disengaged until it was 'Let's go boys' and tap the pads and out you go, which is a lot less draining.

"Marty has the great ability to engage himself when the situation demands it. In some ways the shutout record might be slightly more impressive to me than the wins, because it tells me he had the mental capacity to never lose focus. Marty will tell you he thinks of the first five minutes, then the next

No goalie in the long history of the NHL has had the opportunity
to raise his stick in victory more than Martin Brodeur.

five minutes. If he ever let down, I bet he would have lost 20 of those shutouts."

There's as much room for debate about the most prolific goaltender of all-time as there is between Brodeur's pads and the post. Patrick Roy, with 74 fewer regular season wins, is caught flush in the net in comparison, but even Brodeur suggests somebody as good as Mike Bossy could shoot all day at Roy's status as the greatest *post-season* goaltender and never find a hole in the argument. Brodeur, who is second in all-time playoff wins with 99, marvels at Roy's 151.

"Nobody is going to touch that," Brodeur said, "especially in an era where dynasties are less likely to be started.

"I think I have had pretty good success – won three Stanley Cups, went to another semifinal and a final – and I'm still (many) wins away from him. In playoff shutouts (23) we're tied, that's one I can break, but that win number is crazy. I would have to win three more Stanley Cups and I don't have that many years."

A big part of Brodeur's success stems from the fact he avoided major injuries for much of his career, finally getting bit by arm and knee ailments over the past few seasons. At one point he started 70 or more games in 10 consecutive seasons.

"It's pretty amazing how healthy I was and to be on a good team practically every year," he said. "I took a lot of pride in that streak when it was alive, but at the end it's the wins; that's what the goalie is all about."

Brodeur's wins record will always be celebrated as his pinnacle achievement, but not far behind is topping Sawchuk's record of 103 career shutouts, which was thought for decades to be unbreakable.

"Shutouts are as much about your teammates wanting to sacrifice, not going up ice to get a sixth goal when we were winning 5-0," Brodeur said. "Of course, you still have to stop a few, too. Brian Boucher, five straight shutouts, I'm not going to touch that one.

"But I guess I've had a pretty good run." ∎ Jay Greenberg

◄ Martin Brodeur's swift glove time and time again left shooters at a loss.

MARTIN BRODEUR
OFFICIAL NHL RECORDS

GAMES APPEARED IN BY A GOALTENDER, CAREER: **1,132**

MINUTES PLAYED BY A GOALTENDER, CAREER: **66,636**

MINUTES PLAYED BY A GOALTENDER, ONE SEASON: **4,696:33, 2006-07**

SHUTOUTS, CAREER: **116**

WINS, CAREER: **625**

30-OR-MORE WIN SEASONS BY A GOALTENDER: **13***

CONSECUTIVE 30-OR-MORE WIN SEASONS BY A GOALTENDER:
12, 1995-2007

40-OR-MORE WIN SEASONS BY A GOALTENDER: **8**

CONSECUTIVE 40-OR-MORE WIN SEASONS BY A GOALTENDER:
3, 2005-2008*

WINS BY A GOALTENDER IN ONE SEASON: **48, 2006-07**

SHUTOUTS IN PLAYOFFS, CAREER: **23***

SHUTOUTS, ONE PLAYOFF YEAR: **7, 2003**

SHUTOUTS, ONE PLAYOFF SERIES: **3, 1995 vs. Boston***

*TIED

MONTREAL CANADIENS

When you thumb through the NHL's record book, it's kind of ridiculous, really. Between the regular season and playoffs, Wayne Gretzky's name appears at the top 55 times. Fifty-five frickin' times. So at least we know who holds the record for most NHL records.

That tends to stick out a little bit. But there's also something that's conspicuous by its absence. For an organization that has historically put on display some of the most mind-blowing individual talent and possessed the most dominant teams in the history of the game, there are surprisingly few Montreal Canadiens among the NHL's individual standard bearers.

When it comes to individual records, most of them actually belong to Habs goaltender George Hainsworth, who was once described by hockey historian Eric Zweig as, "one of those dumpy guys whom it would be impossible to believe he could be great at anything. He looks like he's 50 when he's 30."

Hainsworth, who played in an era when scoring a goal was cause for a major celebration because forward passing was prohibited, holds the regular season record for most shutouts in a season (22 in 1928-29, one for each Montreal victory that season), and the playoff mark for the longest shutout sequence (270:08 in 1930). Hainsworth also owns the two best single-season goals-against averages in history, but neither is officially recognized as a record.

Most of the other records held by a Canadien came courtesy Joe Malone, who scored five goals in a game three times during his rookie season of 1917-18, including in his first-ever NHL game (to be fair, everyone was a rookie in '17-18 as it was the league's inaugural campaign). Malone scored 44 goals in 20 games that season, an average of 2.2 per game. For those of you keeping track at home, that means Joe Malone scored more goals per game all by himself than the New Jersey Devils scored as a team in 2010-11. And then, of course, there's Henri Richard, whose 11 Stanley Cups as a player is the most in NHL history. Patrick Roy has a couple of high-water career milestones, but those are split between the Canadiens and the Colorado Avalanche.

Bob Gainey helped add another Stanley Cup to the Montreal Canadiens' resume when his team upended the Rangers in five games in the 1979 championship series.

But that's pretty much it. No Rocket Richard, Guy Lafleur, Jean Beliveau, Doug Harvey, Howie Morenz, Larry Robinson, Jacques Plante or Ken Dryden. We're just going out on a limb here, but we're pretty sure these guys will take their combined 50 Stanley Cups over a prominent place in the NHL record book.

They are there, however. You just can't see their names. For that, you'd have to look at the team records section and read between the lines. Because for all their individual élan, the Canadiens have always been about the collective. And even then, it's not as though Montreal has rewritten the record book from a team perspective. But it owns just about every record that really, really matters.

The thing that is most impressive about the Habs records is that they're likely never to be broken. At the very least they assuredly won't fall in the lifetime of anyone reading this.

Can you see any team winning the Stanley Cup five times in a row anytime soon? The Detroit Red Wings have won four Cups in 13 seasons and they're considered a dynasty. No team has been able to string more than two Cups together since 1983 and we're supposed to expect one to go out and win six?

It's not happening, not in today's NHL where the league is obsessed with parity and winning the Stanley Cup is such a monumental achievement it's next to impossible to even summon the motivation to do it consecutively. One and done seems to be the mantra of the new NHL and there's nothing on the horizon to prompt anyone to expect that to change anytime soon.

It's true teams had to win only two series, a total of eight games, to win the Stanley Cup in the 1950s and compared to the battle of attrition that is the modern day playoffs that seems like child's play. But consider this: If it were so easy to win the Stanley Cup back then, why wasn't everybody doing it? The fact no team in the NHL could even place a one-year dent in the Habs' armor is proof enough they are full marks for their record.

And then there is the grand daddy of them all: The Canadiens 24 Stanley Cups.

Think about it. In order to even tie that record, the Boston Bruins will have to win every Stanley Cup through 2014-15. Is there anyone who believes they have a snowball's chance in Hades to even come close to accomplishing that? Is there anyone who even thinks the Bruins will have enough in the tank to win the Stanley Cup again in 2012?

Didn't think so.

But it's more than just that. Far more. The 1970s team that won four straight Cups might have even been better. For that matter, the outfit that won four Cups in five seasons in the 1960s might

Guy Lafleur, with all his flash and dash, was a first-team NHL all-star for six consecutive seasons to close out the 1970s.

have been the best collective of them all. But it was the 1970s dynasty that put its indelible mark on the record book and the one that is recognized among almost any credible hockey observer as the best team of all-time.

In 1976-77, on the strength of a 60-8-12 record, that team managed to reel off 132 points during the regular season. The only team able to come within striking distance of that benchmark since is the 1995-96 Red Wings, who fell one point short with the benefit of two more games.

Furthermore, the highest number of points any team has earned since, following the lockout season, the league mandated there must be a winner of every game is the Red Wings, who fell eight points short in 2005-06.

How many more points do you figure the Canadiens would have picked up if the schedule had been 82 games instead of 80 and if they had enjoyed the benefit of overtime and a shootout? Think about it. They tied 12 games that season and they had two of the league's top three scorers in Guy Lafleur and Steve Shutt. But get this. Their 387 goals were 48 more than the next highest scoring team, which averages out to more than a half a goal per game. You don't think the Canadiens would have been good for a few more goals in overtime or the shootout? Even if they had gone .500 in extra time that season, they'd have 138 points.

Nobody's catching them on that one either.

That season, the Canadiens also set the low-water mark for losses with eight. In fact, the Canadiens have the four lowest loss totals in the history of the game, all of them recorded during the 1970s. The same goes for road losses in a season. The Canadiens actually lost seven games away from the Montreal Forum in 1976-77, one fewer than they lost on the road in 1972-73 and 1974-75, as well as the same number of losses they posted on the road a year later.

Those six road losses actually aren't the official NHL record, but they are the low-water mark for a minimum 70-game season. None to worry, though, the Canadiens team that lost just three road games in 1928-29 (Hainsworth's shutout-setting season) during a 44-game schedule has that mark locked down, too.

And then there is the grand daddy of them all. The Canadiens have won a total of 24 Stanley Cups in their 100-plus-year history, 23 as members of the NHL. (Interesting fact: The Stanley Cup has been awarded 125 times since 1892-93 and a Montreal team has won it on 43 occasions. Along with the Canadiens, the Maroons, Wanderers, Shamrocks, Victorias and Montreal Amateur Athletic Association have also won the Cup.)

The thing that is most impressive about the Habs records is that they're likely never to be broken.

The Canadiens also hold, by a large margin, records for most appearances in the Stanley Cup final (32), consecutive final appearances (10) and seasons in the playoffs (79). In order for those records to be usurped, the following will have to happen.

The Toronto Maple Leafs, who haven't won a Stanley Cup in 44 years, will have to win 12 more before the Canadiens earn another one. Perhaps it's more reasonable to suggest the Detroit Red Wings will win 14 more before the Habs win one.

The Red Wings will have to appear in the Stanley Cup final another nine times and either the Vancouver Canucks or Boston Bruins will have to get to the final each season for another decade. The Bruins, meanwhile, will have to appear in the playoffs another 24 times without the Canadiens making it even once.

When you put it like that, it looks pretty much impossible. Sure, the Canadiens made almost all of their hay in a six-team league, but they're the only ones who did it. And for that, they will continue to go down as the greatest franchise in the history of the NHL. ▌Ken Campbell

One is left to wonder how high Ken Dryden's numbers would have reached had he not walked away from the game at age 31.

MONTREAL CANADIENS OFFICIAL NHL RECORDS

POINTS, ONE SEASON: **132, 1976-77 (80 GP)**

FEWEST LOSSES, ONE SEASON: **5*, 1943-44 (50 GP)**

FEWEST HOME LOSSES, ONE SEASON: **0*, 1943-44 (25 GP)**

FEWEST ROAD LOSSES, ONE SEASON: **3, 1928-29 (22 GP)**

FEWEST LOSSES, ONE SEASON (MIN. 70-GAME SCHEDULE):
8, 1976-77 (80 GP)

FEWEST HOME LOSSES, ONE SEASON (MIN. 70-GAME SCHEDULE):
1 1976-77 (40 GP)

FEWEST ROAD LOSSES, ONE SEASON (MIN. 70-GAME SCHEDULE):
6 1972-73, (39 GP); 1974-75, (40 GP); 1977-78, (40 GP)

CONSECUTIVE HOME GAMES WITHOUT A LOSS, ONE SEASON:
34, 1976-1977 (28-0-6)

CONSECUTIVE ROAD GAMES WITHOUT A LOSS, ONE SEASON:
23, 1974-1975 (14-0-9)

CONSECUTIVE HOME GAMES WITHOUT A LOSS, INCLUDING PLAYOFFS:
38, 1976-1977 (28-0-6; 4-0)

CONSECUTIVE ROAD GAMES WITHOUT A LOSS, INCLUDING PLAYOFFS:
13*, 1979-80 (6-0-4; 3-0)

CONSECUTIVE GAMES WITHOUT A LOSS, INCLUDING PLAYOFFS:
24, 1979-80 (15-0-6; 3-0).

GOALS, ONE TEAM, ONE GAME: **16, Mar. 3, 1920 vs. Quebec**

GOALS, BOTH TEAMS, ONE GAME: **21, Jan. 10, 1920 vs. Toronto***

FASTEST THREE GOALS FROM START OF PERIOD, BOTH TEAMS:
1:05, March 11, 1989 vs. Hartford (2nd period)

FEWEST GOALS AGAINST, ONE SEASON (MIN. 70-GAME SCHEDULE):
131, 1955-56 (70 GP)*

_____

LOWEST GOALS-AGAINST AVERAGE, ONE SEASON: **0.98, 1928-29**

_____

SHUTOUTS, ONE SEASON: **22, 1928-29 (44 GP)**

_____

STANLEY CUPS: **23, 1924, '30, '31, '44, '46, '53, '56, '57, '58, '59, '60, '65, '66, '68, '69, '71, '73, '76, '77, '78, '79, '86, '93**

_____

CONSECUTIVE STANLEY CUP CHAMPIONSHIPS: **5, 1956-1960**

_____

FINAL SERIES APPEARANCES: **32**

_____

CONSECUTIVE FINAL SERIES APPEARANCES: **10, 1951-1960**

_____

YEARS IN PLAYOFFS: **79**

_____

OVERTIME WINS, ONE TEAM, ONE PLAYOFF YEAR: **10, 1993**

_____

OVERTIME WINS AT HOME, ONE TEAM, ONE PLAYOFF YEAR: **4, 1993***

_____

OVERTIME WINS ON THE ROAD, ONE TEAM, ONE PLAYOFF YEAR: **6, 1993**

_____

OVERTIME LOSSES, ONE TEAM, ONE PLAYOFF YEAR: **4, 1951***

_____

CONSECUTIVE WINS, ONE TEAM, ONE PLAYOFF YEAR: **11, 1993***

_____

GOALS, BOTH TEAMS, TWO-GAME SERIES: **17, 1918 vs. Toronto**

_____

FEWEST GOALS, BOTH TEAMS, THREE-GAME SERIES: **7, 1929 vs. Boston***

_____

GOALS, ONE TEAM, ONE PERIOD: **7, March 3, 1944 vs. Toronto (3rd period)**

_____

SHORTHAND GOALS, ONE TEAM, ONE PERIOD: **2, three times***

_____

FASTEST FOUR GOALS, ONE TEAM: **2:35, March 30, 1944 vs. Toronto**

_____

FASTEST FIVE GOALS, ONE TEAM: **3:36, March 30, 1944 vs. Toronto**

_____

SHORTEST OVERTIME: **0:09, May 18, 1986 vs. Calgary**

_____

OVERTIME GAMES, ONE SERIES: **5, 1951 vs. Toronto**

_____

*TIED

Quick Off The Draw

GOALS BY A ROOKIE
[TEEMU SELANNE: 76]

Because hockey players are some of the most humble athletes in all of sport, you won't find too many of them willing to suggest the record they hold will take an extremely long time to be broken.

But veteran star right winger Teemu Selanne – one of hockey's best ambassadors and a man who would brag only if forced to at gunpoint – will tell you the mark he is most famous for won't be challenged in the next couple years – if ever.

That's because a fresh-faced Selanne scored a whopping 76 times for the Winnipeg Jets in 1992-93, setting the standard for goals in a season by a rookie. On second thought, "setting" is too delicate a word for what he accomplished. Selanne demolished the previous record of 53 in a season, established by Islanders Hall of Famer Mike Bossy during the 1977-78 campaign.

For some perspective, Alex Ovechkin scored 52 times in his rookie season. The leading rookie scorer in the 2010-11 season was Islanders right winger Michael Grabner, who had 34 goals, less than half of what Selanne netted in his first year. More perspective: only three NHLers in history have ever scored more than 76 goals in any season – Brett Hull and Mario Lemieux and Wayne Gretzky, who did it twice.

"In my time, it was whoever scores more goals wins."
Teemu Selanne

None of this is to say Selanne is some superhuman specimen scientifically engineered in his homeland of Finland to be an unstoppable force. The truth is, like so many of the greats, Selanne was the beneficiary of fate. He entered the NHL just prior to the dawn of the defense-first, obstruction-heavy, Dead Puck Era (which lasted roughly from 1994 to 2004). As such,

the man known as the Finnish Flash had the type of creative license and opportunities on offense that no player has had ever since.

"Absolutely, I was in the right time and the right place to get that," Selanne said. "The game was totally different when I started in the NHL. The biggest difference now is the attitude of the teams. Now, teams say, 'there's no way we're going to give up more than two or three goals a game.' But in my time, it was, 'whoever scores more goals wins.' The whole mindset was different and that's why there was so many high-scoring games back then."

Selanne demolished the previous record of 53 rookie goals in a season.

After that record-breaking freshman campaign – which (surprise, surprise) won him the Calder Trophy as the league's best rookie – Selanne's goal total never again reached the same staggering heights. He did have 50-goal seasons for two straight years with the Mighty Ducks of Anaheim in 1996-97 (51) and 1997-98 (52), but then settled in as a consistent scoring threat averaging nearly 30 goals per season. In the more modern, defense-focused NHL, that's quite the accomplishment.

"It was a lot of fun in my first year, because there was a lot of goals – not just for me, but for the whole league," said Selanne, who by the end of 2010-11 had career offensive totals of 637 goals and 1,340 points in 1,259 games. "Even in the games we didn't score that many goals, there was nearly double the number of scoring chances we have now. That's a big difference from the way it is today." ▌ Adam Proteau

◄ Who can forget Teemu Selanne shooting down his glove in celebration after breaking Mike Bossy's rookie goal-scoring record?

CONSECUTIVE GAMES WITH A GOAL TO START CAREER
[EVGENI MALKIN, 6]

When the Pittsburgh Penguins selected Evgeni Malkin second overall in the 2004 draft, they knew they'd have to wait a while for him to come overseas. It was worth it.

The big Russian's NHL debut was put off until the 2006-07 season because of an international transfer dispute, but once Malkin got on NHL ice it didn't take him long to make up for lost time.

In his first half-dozen games Malkin set the record for a goal-scoring streak to start a career, totalling seven goals and 11 points. His streak started with a goal against legendary netminder Martin Brodeur and was snapped against the San Jose Sharks in a contest that also stopped the Pens' longest winning streak in five years, at five.

Malkin finished his first campaign with 33 goals and 85 points, earning him the Calder Trophy as rookie of the year.

Evgeni Malkin took the league
by storm after coming over from
Russia, winning the Calder Trophy
in his first season and the Art Ross
and Conn Smythe in his third.

GOALS BY A ROOKIE DEFENSEMAN
[BRIAN LEETCH, 23]

As a 21-year-old rookie, Brian Leetch tallied an NHL record for first-year defensemen with 23 goals in 1988-89 for the New York Rangers. For Leetch it was a case of the right player in the right situation.

In an interview with THN, Leetch said his first coach with New York, Michel Bergeron, gave him the liberty to freelance on the ice: "It was great for me as a young player because I wasn't going out there afraid of making mistakes."

Bergeron trusted Leetch in all situations, reflected by the blueliner's eight power play goals and three tallies on the penalty kill. Leetch finished 1988-89 with 71 points, second all-time for freshmen rearguards, and took home the Calder Trophy as the league's top rookie.

FASTEST HAT TRICK
[BILL MOSIENKO, 21 SECONDS]

On the first day of spring, 1952, the last-place Chicago Black Hawks took the Friday train to Toronto for a Saturday night game against the Maple Leafs. Nine-year Hawks vet Bill Mosienko was wrapping up his best offensive season since his rookie year and, having the night off, decided to look up an old friend. They got together for a

It's rare when a player scores three goals in 60 minutes, but Bill Mosienko's trio of tallies against the New York Rangers on March 23, 1952 came in 21 seconds.

drink, a meal and a gab session that rainy evening, then relaxed around a collection of hockey books.

"We were thumbing through the NHL record book," Mosienko recalled a few days later, "and I remarked how nice it would be to have my name in there with some of the hockey greats. But I just figured it would never happen – and then it did, 48 hours later."

After the Saturday night in Toronto, a game in which Mosienko scored two goals, including the winner, in a 3-2 upset over the third-place Maple Leafs, the Black Hawks left immediately for the season finale in New York on Sunday, March 23, 1952.

Because it was a match of two non-playoff teams, the Rangers closed the mezzanine and balcony at Madison Square Garden, leaving just the arena bowl open for about 6,000 spectators.

"That had to be the smallest crowd in the history of the New York Rangers," said long-time hockey journalist Stan Fischler, who was 19 at the time and vice-president of the Rangers fan club. "It was a meaningless game not seen by a lot of people. The Rangers even put in their third-string goalie because Chuck Rayner and Emile Francis were worn down."

New York held a comfortable 6-2 third-period lead when Mosienko went about putting himself in the record books with some of the hockey greats.

He took a Gus Bodnar setup and shot past 20-year-old third-stringer Lorne Anderson at 6:09 of the third. Bodnar won the next faceoff, ragged the puck a few seconds, then fed a streaking Mosienko, who had split the defense. Mosienko beat Anderson at 6:20. On the next faceoff, Bodnar won the puck over to left winger George Gee, who laid a timing pass to Mosienko for another goal at 6:30 to narrow the score to 6-5 – and set the record for the fastest hat trick in NHL history.

> *"We were thumbing through the NHL record book and I remarked how nice it would be to have my name in there with some of the hockey greats."*
>
> Bill Mosienko

Remarkably, Chicago coach Ebbie Goodfellow kept the Bodnar line on the ice for another post-goal faceoff against the reeling Rangers.

"Bodnar won the draw again," Fischler recalled, "somehow got the puck to 'Mosie' and he took a shot that rang off the post. It could have easily been four goals in 28 seconds."

Legend has it, when Mosienko skated to the bench after that shot off the iron, Goodfellow barked at him: "What the heck happened? You in a slump?"

Chicago scored two more goals and went on to win 7-6. For Anderson, it was the third and final game of his career. He spent most of that 1951-52 season with the Eastern League's New York Rovers, but after the five-goal shell-shocking in the third period, he didn't return to pro hockey.

"The entire feat seemed to slip by under the radar," Fischler said. "In those days, there were no post-game press conferences, there was no TV. And because it was a nothing game, there wasn't much of a media report from the game."

The passage of time, however, has turned Mosienko's three goals in 21 seconds into a mythical achievement destined never to be broken. Scores of players since have scored two goals in 17 seconds or less, but none have been able to eclipse the 21-second hat trick.

The closest anyone has come to that since is 44 seconds by Jean Beliveau in 1955. Mosienko's three goals in 21 seconds bettered Carl Liscombe's 1938 record of three goals in 64 seconds.

Said Mosienko, inducted into the Hall of Fame in 1965: "It was something to dream about." ▌Brian Costello

FASTEST PLAYOFF OVERTIME GOAL
[BRIAN SKRUDLAND, 9 SECONDS]

005

During a Stanley Cup final with unexpected teams, an unexpected record was set.

Patrick Roy's gallant goaltending, on display throughout the playoffs, wasn't needed past the third period in Game 2. A mere nine seconds into overtime Brian Skrudland tapped in a beautiful fake-shot pass from Mike McPhee past Calgary's Mike Vernon, giving the Canadiens a 3-2 win May 18, 1986.

The second assist on the play was one of rookie Claude Lemieux's 16 playoff points, second only to Mats Naslund's 19 when Canadiens captain Bob Gainey raised the Cup.

The goal was a rarity for Skrudland, who scored just twice in 20 games during the '85-86 playoffs. During his career, the Peace River, Alta., native totalled 124 goals and 343 points in 881 games.

006

CONSECUTIVE GAMES WITHOUT A LOSS TO START A CAREER
[PATRICK LALIME, 16]

Examine the beginning of Patrick Lalime's NHL career and you'll find Ken Wregget all over the place. After all, it was Wregget who Lalime replaced in net for the Penguins rookie goalie's first NHL win on Dec. 6, 1996 against Washington.

But it was also Wregget who took the 'L' a month earlier in Lalime's first NHL appearance. Though Lalime played more than 29 minutes against the Rangers that night – giving up three goals in the process – Wregget was tagged with the loss because the Pens were trailing when he was pulled. Had the Pens taken the lead at any point, Lalime's record 16-game unbeaten streak to start his NHL career may not have happened.

By the end of the Lalime-led streak the Penguins were breathing down the necks of the top-seeded Flyers.

And truthfully, the 14-0-2 run could not have occurred at a better time. Starter Tom Barrasso played just five games that season due to a shoulder injury and Wregget followed him to the IR on Boxing Day with a pulled hamstring. Despite boasting two of the decade's best players in Mario Lemieux and Jaromir Jagr (with Petr Nedved, Kevin Hatcher and Ron Francis also on the roster), the Penguins were a mediocre team through the early going, hovering around .500 and holding down seventh place in the Eastern Conference. By the end of the Lalime-led streak – broken by Colorado on Adam Deadmarsh's power play game-winner on Jan. 23 – the Penguins were breathing

Avoiding a loss for his first 16 games, Patrick Lalime had a brilliant start to his career.

down the necks of the top-seeded Flyers and sitting third overall in the NHL. At the time, Lalime was being compared, at least stylistically, to Patrick Roy.

Lalime finished the season on a down note with an overall record of 21-12-2 and never replicated St. Patrick's success in the post-season (they fell to Philadelphia in five games that year with Wregget in net), but he'll always have that terrific debut that has yet to be matched.

FASTEST GOAL TO START A CAREER
[DAVE CHRISTIAN, 7 SECONDS]

007

For Dave Christian, the memory is of a whirlwind week.

In one moment, Christian was in Lake Placid, N.Y., celebrating the most improbable of victories – the 1980 Olympic gold-medal victory over Finland after the U.S. upset the powerhouse Soviets in the "Miracle on Ice." A week later, after celebrating "Dave Christian Day" in his tiny hometown of Warroad, Minn., Christian slipped on an NHL sweater for the first time, three hours northwest of home in Winnipeg, Manitoba.

"There were butterflies and nerves in the pre-game, all throughout warmups," Christian said. "My first shift, I go out there and there were butterflies and nerves."

When the puck dropped, however, those "butterflies and nerves" subsided immediately. Seven seconds later, Christian, with arms raised, remembers thinking: "Well, that was pretty lucky."

Yes, it took seven measly seconds for Christian to score during his first NHL shift – a record that stands today. Was the NHL really that easy?

"No," Christian said, laughing. "I didn't think that."

Christian, a defenseman for Herb Brooks' Team USA squad, was centering Kris Manery and Morris Lukowich during that first shift with the Jets.

"Second shift of the game, Mike Veisor was the goaltender for Chicago, offensive-zone faceoff to his left," Christian recalled. "We won the faceoff, the puck went back to the point and I went to the front of the net. The defenseman, Ross Cory, shot the puck. The rebound came right to me and I shot it in."

Seven seconds in, Dave Christian, with arms raised, remembers thinking: "Well, that was pretty lucky."

The week was as well-scripted as Christian could have imagined. After winning gold, Christian returned home for a few days, then went to Grand Forks, N.D., to seek advice from Fighting Sioux coach Gino Gasparini. Jets GM John Ferguson had driven to Warroad immediately after the Olympics to offer Christian his first NHL contract. The Jets had drafted Christian 40th overall the previous summer and Christian wondered if this was the right time to leave school.

"I went back to Grand Forks, thought about it for a couple days and just realized having played for that entire year at the level we had played at (with Team USA), I thought it would be best to move on," Christian said. "I don't know that I got to enjoy winning the gold, but maybe that was good. Things happened so fast. We had that elation and then at 20 years old, there was a lot of life left. If I was going to make a career out of hockey, it was probably the best time just to get on with it."

"I do miss the game. I miss the locker room. I miss the camaraderie of having teammates."

Dave Christian

Christian went on to play more than 1,000 NHL games with Winnipeg, Washington, Boston, St. Louis and Chicago, scoring 340 goals and 773 points. Along the way, he captained the Jets, topped 40 goals and 80 points one year for the Caps and reached a Stanley Cup final with the Bruins.

"I wasn't unhappy with the career that I had," Christian said. "We all have a goal of winning the Stanley Cup. It didn't happen. But overall, yeah, I'm happy with how it went. I had a blast."

Christian comes from a sprawling hockey family. His father, Bill, and uncle, Roger, won gold at the 1960 Olympics with Bill scoring the winning goal. Another uncle, Gord, played in the 1956 Olympics and his nephews, Brock Nelson and Jordy Christian, play collegiately at North Dakota and St. Cloud State.

In the late '90s and early 2000s, Christian coached Fargo-Moorhead of the United States League. He also spent time coaching bantam girls in the Moorhead (Minn.) Youth Hockey Association, the organization that helped produce NHLers such as Matt Cullen and Jason Blake.

These days, Christian works for an insolating glass factory in Fargo, N.D. He's completely out of hockey, playing at most one or two charity games a year.

His family even sold Christian Brothers Hockey Company, which is now owned in part by NHLer Dustin Byfuglien and his stepfather, Dale Smedsmo. Christian says he misses hockey "every day."

"I miss the playing, I don't miss the training," said Christian, who led the 1980 U.S. team in assists with eight. "But I do miss the game. I miss the locker room. I miss the camaraderie of having teammates. I enjoyed every minute. It went fast, that's for sure."

Surprisingly, Christian's highlight wasn't the 1980 Olympics or scoring the fastest goal in NHL history into one's first shift.

It was when he was 17, his senior year of high school, when he played for the Warroad Lakers, an old senior and intermediate league team that played Canadian teams in events such as the

Hardy Cup and Allan Cup. One of his teammates on the club was his father.

"It was very special, probably the thing I enjoyed the most," Christian said. "My dad is a big reason why I played. I don't ever remember having any pressure to play. I don't remember ever learning how to skate, so I evidently must have been in the rink pretty young. I evidently must have loved it." ▌ Michael Russo

008

FASTEST TWO GOALS BY A TEAM
[MINNESOTA WILD, 3 SECONDS]

Think of the Wild's early days and scoring doesn't pop to mind. But on Jan. 21, 2004, Minny's offense went off... for a very short span, anyway. Hosting the Chicago Blackhawks, Minnesota's Jim Dowd beat Craig Anderson on his own rebound at 19:44 of the third period to break a 2-2 tie. Three seconds later, Richard Park shot the puck off the faceoff into an empty net to seal a 4-2 win. Using that time span in the equation, the Wild's offense would have rolled along at 1,200 goals-per-game, a slight uptick from their real average of 2.29 that season.

Pucks & Bucks

009

GOALS AHEAD OF SECOND PLACE IN A SCORING RACE
[BRETT HULL, 35]

Brett Hull is a lot of things – Hart Trophy winner, first ballot Hall of Famer and one of the greatest goal scorers in hockey history – but frequently caught off guard? Not so much.

When informed he is the holder of one of hockey's greatest records, however, Hull can't hide his surprise.

"Are you sure," asked a skeptical Hull. "You're telling me that there's a record that Gretzky doesn't own?"

Playing with the St. Louis Blues in 1990-91, Hull scored an NHL-best 86 goals, an amazing 35 more than his closest competition in the trio of Cam Neely, Theo Fleury and Steve Yzerman at 51. That 35-goal gap between the first- and second-place finishers in the goal-scoring race remains an NHL record and a mark that figures to be in the record book for many years to come.

"Wow, I never knew that," Hull said. "I thought for sure that Wayne held all the goal-scoring records."

The 1991 Hart Trophy winner, Hull potted a single season total of 86 goals that has only been bettered by one player in NHL history – the aforementioned Wayne Gretzky – and is still the most ever scored by a right winger. Sandwiched between a 72-goal season the year before and a 70-goal season the next, his three consecutive seasons of 70-plus goals have only ever been bettered by one player – once again, Gretzky.

When asked for the secret to his success in those years, Hull is quick to credit his center at the time, Adam Oates.

"He was the perfect complement to me," Hull said. "I loved to score goals and Adam loved to set up goals. I consider him a genius when it comes to offensive creativity, right up there with Gretzky. In my opinion he's the most underrated player to ever play the game."

Some of the Blues uniforms Brett
Hull was forced to don in St. Louis
were unholy, but his one-timer in
any garb was god-like.

'Hull and Oates,' as they were popularly known, enjoyed a rare chemistry both on and off the ice. On the road they roomed together, ate their meals together and all the while talked about hockey. They bought homes close to one another in St. Louis and, according to Hull, "were on the same wavelength." Their on-ice chemistry was honed to the point they didn't have to even communicate with each other to know what the other wanted to do.

"'You're telling me that there's a record that Gretzky doesn't own?"
Brett Hull

For three years, Hull and Oates reigned as hockey's most feared offensive duo. Hull led the NHL in goals all three years, while Oates enjoyed three consecutive seasons in the league's top 10 scorers, while at the same time finishing third, second and fourth in assists.

The incredible duo was broken up on Feb. 7, 1992 when Oates was traded to the Boston Bruins. Hull continued on for more than a decade, scoring goals and cementing his Hall of Fame legacy, but he never again reached the heights of 70 goals in a season.

"If Adam doesn't get traded, it's scary to think of how many more goals I would have scored," said Hull, now the executive VP of the Dallas Stars. "I might even have been able to have taken a shot at Gretzky's record."

As it stands, Hull ended his career in third place on the NHL's all-time goal-scoring list (Gordie Howe is No. 2), but right now he can hardly wait for the next time he shares a round of golf with his good friend, Gretzky.

"I finally have one over on him," Hull said. "Who would have thought that I would have a spot in the record book ahead of him?" ∎ Todd Denault

Jaromir Jagr

MONEY MADE IN A CAREER
[JAROMIR JAGR, $98 MILLION]

010

At some point during Jaromir Jagr's storied NHL career, he came to realize he could afford a decent haircut. After years of rocking arguably the greatest hockey mullet, he took some of his all-time high $98,038,851 career earnings and chopped off the locks.

Jagr's spot at the top will be toppled soon, however. Nicklas Lidstrom – who's only a stride behind at $94,165,000 – will take the No. 1 spot when the 41-year-old laces'em up for 2011-12. (At the rate Lidstrom is going, he could probably play for another decade.)

The biggest single contract? That belongs to Alex Ovechkin. He inked a 13-year, $124-million extension with the Washington Capitals that began in 2008-09. That deal expires in the summer of 2021 when he's 35.

011

OLDEST SCORING CHAMPION
[BILL COOK, 36]

Recognized as one of the greatest right wingers of all-time, Bill Cook was the centerpiece of the early New York Rangers teams. A two-time scoring champion in the professional Western Canada League, Cook was the first player officially signed by the Rangers in 1926 as they were preparing for their inaugural NHL season. In fact, 'The Original Ranger' not only became the first captain in team history, but he also scored the Blueshirts' first goal, on Nov. 16, 1926, in a 1-0 win over the Montreal Maroons.

Cook, his little brother 'Bun' and Frank Boucher made up the famed 'Bread Line' that was one of the early NHL's most fearsome threesomes. In that first season, Cook led the league with 37 points, but was runner-up for the Hart Trophy to the Canadiens' Herb Gardiner.

> *Bill Cook not only became the first captain in Rangers history, but he also scored their first ever goal.*

But while Cook and the 'Bread Line' led the Rangers to four Stanley Cup final appearances and two championships over the following six seasons, the elder brother didn't win his second scoring title until 1932-33 when he registered 50 points in 48 games as a 36-year-old. While he once again finished second place for the Hart Trophy, this time behind Boston's Eddie Shore, Cook capped off the season by scoring the NHL's first Stanley Cup-winning overtime goal.

As small consolation for missing out on MVP honors despite leading the league in scoring, Cook snagged the record for the league's oldest scoring champion, a title he holds to this day.

Gordie Howe won the scoring title in 1962-63 as a 34-year-old to make him the oldest Art Ross winner in the modern era, which is fitting since Cook and Howe played the same physical, power-forward game.

In fact, the Toronto *Star*'s Milt Dunnell once wrote: "When Gordie Howe came into the league, old-timers said: 'There's another Bill Cook.'"

◄ Bill Cook, 1947.

012

CONSECUTIVE GAMES SOLD OUT
[COLORADO AVALANCHE, 487]

F or the NHL, the relocation from Quebec City to Denver could not have gone smoother. The Avalanche hoisted the Stanley Cup in their first year in Colorado and in doing so managed to build a considerable fan base in the mile-high city right out of the gate.

The consecutive sellout streak began during just the eighth game in Avs history, Nov. 9, 1995, against the Dallas Stars. The streak extended beyond the NHL lockout, lasting 3,994 days and coming to a halt at 487 games on Oct. 16, 2006 versus the Chicago Blackhawks.

As the Avalanche tumbled from the Western Conference's elite, attendance at the Pepsi Center also began to dwindle. Colorado ranked 10th in average attendance in 2005-06, but by 2010-11 ranked 25th as the team limped to a 29th-place finish.

DRAFT PICKS IN ONE YEAR
[ST. LOUIS BLUES, 31]

013

Had the TV show *Hoarders* existed five decades ago, there's a good chance the St. Louis Blues would have starred in the summer of 1978. That year they stockpiled a mind-boggling 31 draft picks, unheard of by today's standards.

After losing their second round pick after signing restricted free agent Rod Seiling from Toronto and trading their fourth-rounder, the Blues obtained 19 picks for cash between Rounds 9 and 14. As a response, the NHL banned teams from paying money for draft slots following the '78 derby.

The prospect-palooza didn't go as well as the Blues had hoped as only five of their 31 picks, four more than the Montreal Canadiens used the year before, made the NHL and none had a big impact with St. Louis.

Wayne Babych, selected third overall, scored 54 goals in 1981-82, but managed just 48 in three seasons after. Jim Nill, 89th overall, played 61 games before being traded to Vancouver during his rookie season, while Paul MacLean, 109th overall, played once before being traded to Winnipeg where he scored 101 points in 1984-85. MacLean was reacquired in 1989 and played parts of two seasons before retiring. Goaltender Bob Froese, 160th overall, and defenseman Risto Siltanen, 173rd, never played a game for the Blues, but spent significant time with other NHL teams.

◄ When the times were good in Colorado,
fans of the Avalanche came out in droves.

014

GAMES PLAYED
BY A SET OF SIBLINGS
[SUTTERS, 4,994]

The history of hockey is dotted with successful brother acts. Maurice and Henri Richard and Bill and Bun Cook shared much more than brotherhood, winning Stanley Cups together as teammates before heading to the Hockey Hall of Fame. Henrik and Daniel Sedin came up short of the Cup, but won back-to-back Art Ross Trophies in 2010 and 2011.

Other brother combos competed against one another. Phil Esposito routinely parked himself in brother Tony's slot, Dave and Ken Dryden became the only siblings to stare each other down from opposite creases in 1971 and Wayne and Keith Primeau actually dropped the gloves and fought each other in 1997.

There have also been triple threats: The Bentleys, Hunters, Staals, Stastnys and Plagers were all NHL troikas. The Conachers, Lionel, Roy and Charlie, are the only trio of brothers enshrined in the Hockey Hall of Fame.

But when it comes to NHL siblings, there's never been anything quite like the Sutter clan from Viking, Alta.

Brian, Darryl, Duane, Brent, Rich and Ron Sutter all debuted in the NHL during the late 1970s or early '80s and during a quarter-century span the six brothers played in 4,994 NHL games, scored 1,320 goals and totaled 2,934 points – all NHL records.

As a collective, the brothers' best season was 1984-85, when the six combined for 138 goals and 316 points – another NHL record. But mere numbers only tell part of the Sutter story.

"The Sutters' impact is enormous," said Dean Spiros, author of *Six Shooters: Hockey's Sutter Brothers*. "They have become a brand name for what it means to compete and work at the highest level."

Today, almost a generation after the Sutters stopped playing, scouts continue to scour arenas looking for young prospects who "play like a Sutter" – honest, hard-working players. A "Sutter-type" never coasts or takes a shift off, is the ultimate team player, will take a hit rather than give up the puck, will do the dirty work in the corners and in front of the net, will fight for every square inch of ice and sacrifice statistics for wins.

"The one word that ties all six of them together is respect," Spiros said. "It's a basic principle that guides them in all aspects of their lives. It manifests itself on so many levels in hockey. Respect for the game, their team, their teammates, their opponent; respect for the trainers and equipment managers. And a self-respect that joined with everything else made it impossible to give anything but 100 percent every time that they were on the ice."

The Sutter legacy lives on. Four of the six brothers (Brian, Duane, Darryl and Brent) have been either an NHL coach or GM, while the twins (Rich and Ron) are both NHL scouts. And the next generation of Sutters is emerging. Brandon (Brent's son) is 22 and a two-way center for the Hurricanes. His 23-year-old cousin Brett (Darryl's son) is a left winger who's also in the Carolina organization.

Scouts today continue to scour arenas looking for young prospects who "play like a Sutter."

"For a lot of reasons there probably will never be another story like it," Spiros said. "An interesting aspect to the story that people tend to overlook is that there are seven Sutter boys. Gary is the oldest and his brothers all say Gary had the best talent. His career was sidetracked due to a decision to leave junior hockey to be with a girlfriend. So as amazing as it is that six brothers made the NHL, it could have been seven." ▌Todd Denault

015

MOST EXPENSIVE ARENA TO BUILD
[AMERICAN AIRLINES CENTER, $420 MILLION]

Apparently, they do things bigger in Texas. According to the Internet, which is never wrong, the state is home to the world's largest: spider, rodent, horse, pecan, honky tonk and cowboy boots. And that data was uncovered on just the first page of more than 119,000,000 search hits.

Buried somewhere deeper in the results is American Airlines Center in Dallas, which at a cost of $420 million to construct, is the NHL arena with the steepest price tag. It's also one of the finest facilities in which to watch a game.

Built in 2001, AAC is a multi-purpose venue that seats 18,532 for hockey. It is known for its terrific sightlines and acoustics, but even more so for its killer video technology. Its 1080p high-definition video replay system, installed in 2009, is the first of its kind and the biggest (there's that word again) in any North American arena. There are also giant stadium-sized screens at either end of the rink.

The building has been host to its share of memorable moments, though not yet a Stanley Cup celebration; Dallas won its only NHL title in Buffalo in 1999, two years before AAC opened. The arena was the site of the 55th NHL All-Star Game in 2007, won 12-9 by the Western Conference. It was where Dixie Chicks lead singer Natalie Maines received a death threat following her controversial comments about President George W. Bush. And AAC earned a place in the Guinness Book of World Records for its opening night ribbon-cutting ceremony. The feat? Biggest ribbon, of course.

HIGHEST PERCENTAGE OF A TEAM'S GOALS SCORED
[PAVEL BURE, 29.5%]

016

The old adage that you're only as good as your best player often holds true in hockey, but it's a dangerous game to play if your star pupil has to do all the heavy lifting himself.

Panthers coach Terry Murray leaned heavily on his sole offensive force, Pavel Bure, during the 2000-01 season. The Russian Rocket averaged almost 27 minutes of ice time per game, six more minutes than any other Panther forward.

Russia's flashiest export made the most of his ice time. Bure scored 59 of the Panthers' 200 goals in 2000-01, 29.5 percent of Florida's goals – the highest percentage of team goals scored by one player in NHL history. Bure led the league in goals in 2000-01 with little support from his teammates. Predictably, Bure's one-man show was not enough to carry the Panthers to the playoffs.

Pavel Bure

The Long & Short Of It

TALLEST PLAYER
[ZDENO CHARA, 6-FOOT-9]

017

You call that a record?

Zdeno Chara acknowledges being the tallest player in NHL history at 6-foot-9, but since he didn't actually do anything to earn the distinction except grow, he has a hard time thinking he "set" anything.

"The way I look at it, somebody has to be the tallest and somebody has to be the shortest," said the Boston Bruins defenseman. "It's not something you can control, right?"

Can't argue with that – and since Chara, who is famously obsessive about training, packs 255 pounds onto all that length, only a fool would argue with him, anyway.

Chara learned long ago to work around things he couldn't control – especially the notion that he had a body better suited for sports other than hockey.

"I faced that adversity pretty much my whole time in youth hockey," he said. "It was very frustrating, nerve-wracking, because I wanted to play hockey really bad. It was very complicated, but I'm glad I could do it and become an NHL player."

Chara comes by his athletic genes honestly. His dad, Zdenek, was a 6-foot-2 Greco-Roman wrestler who competed for Czechoslovakia at the 1976 Olympics.

As one of the NHL's premier shutdown defensemen, Chara takes full advantage of his strength, reach and surprising mobility. He has honed his craft over time, first with the Islanders, who drafted him 56th overall in 1996, then with the Senators after being part of the deal that sent Alexei Yashin to Long Island in 2001. In 2006, Chara signed with Boston as a free agent and continued his evolution into one of the best shutdown defensemen in the league, winning the 2009 Norris Trophy. He has one of the most feared shots in the game and also, on occasion, parks his huge frame in front of opposing goalies on the power play.

Behemoth
Zdeno Chara
made 5-foot-10
teammate
Mark Recchi
look child-like
on the ice.

Chara isn't the easiest guy to get suited in proper-fitting gear, but it's not as challenging as one might initially think.

Skates, for instance, aren't a problem. According to Boston equipment manager Keith Robinson, Chara didn't even have the biggest skates on the team in 2010-11. The Bruins' captain wedged his feet into size 11¾ while fellow defenseman Johnny Boychuk (6-foot-2, 225) wore a 12½. Robinson – who grew accustomed to equipping king-sized players when 6-foot-7, 240-pound Hal Gill patrolled Boston's blueline from 1997 to 2006 – has also seen his share of hockey pants as big or bigger than Chara's size large-plus-2. The jersey is 58-plus, to give Chara extra room in the sleeves and chest. When not cut exactly correct, the equipment staff makes alterations.

"Somebody has to be the tallest and somebody has to be the shortest."
Zdeno Chara

The biggest difference between Chara and the average NHL player is his stick. First of all, because of his height, he's given a two-inch allowance over the NHL's standard maximum of 63 inches (players 6-foot-6 and taller are allowed to use a 65-inch stick, provided they make the request).

The shafts of those sticks are as stiff as they come: In 2010-11, the flex on Chara's sticks measured 130 – and that was down from 150 two years earlier. According to Robinson, the flex on the majority of NHL sticks is in the 90-to-95 range.

"To get the velocity he gets into a shot," Robinson said, "the amount of force when he hits the ice just before hitting the puck requires that stiff of a stick."

The shot, of course, is a record-breaker. In 2011, Chara won his fourth straight hardest shot title at the NHL All-Star Game skills competition with a bench-setting blast of 105.9 MPH.

But there is only one "record" Chara is actually interested in: hoisting the Stanley Cup – and he accomplished that in 2011.

"I'll know," Chara said, "the trophy will be raised higher over the ice than it ever was." ▌ Mike Loftus

018

SHORTEST CAREER
BY A GOALIE
[JORDAN SIGALET,
43 SECONDS]

t's a career stat line as intriguing as it is melancholy: one game, one minute, no shots against.

Thus, in his only NHL appearance, goaltender Jordan Sigalet finished the night with a 0.00 goals-against average and, despite the fact the Boston Bruins tried to induce the visiting Lightning into throwing a puck on net, a .000 save percentage.

Sigalet's appearance came in 2005-06, backing up Andrew Raycroft on a January night when normal No. 2 Hannu Toivonen was in the press box with a cast on his foot. When Raycroft tweaked something late in the third, Sigalet got the call. Technically, he played 43 seconds.

It would be his last NHL game. Sigalet, who had been diagnosed with multiple sclerosis in 2004, never made it back to The Show, playing in the minors and Austria the rest of his short pro career. Strangely, his appearance wasn't the last Sigalet to play only one game for the Black and Gold. The following season, defenseman Jonathan Sigalet, Jordan's younger brother, skated in his lone NHL game in an otherwise all-AHL pro career.

Jordan now serves as goaltending coach for the AHL's Abbotsford Heat.

▶ Jordan Sigalet had a very brief taste of the NHL.
So brief, in fact, that he never even faced a shot on goal.

019

LONGEST NON-HYPHENATED SURNAME
[JOHN BRACKENBOROUGH, 14 LETTERS]

His NHL career lasted just seven games with Boston during the 1925-26 season, but the late John Brackenborough, who lived to the ripe old age of 96, managed to get his name into the record book nonetheless.

An eye injury ended his career prematurely, but Brackenborough's 14-letter surname is the longest non-hyphenated name in NHL history.

Although names didn't appear on the back of NHL sweaters until 1971 – and then only for the home team – Brackenborough would have been a tough one to stitch. Today, plenty of hyphenated names come in longer than 14 letters (Drouin-Deslauriers, Letourneau-Leblond, 17 characters), but many are whittled down to one name for sweater purposes.

The record for longest name including first and middle names? Calgary Flames captain Jarome Arthur-Leigh Adekunle Tig Junior Elvis Iginla would surely lead the list.

SHORTHANDED GOALS IN ONE SEASON
[MARIO LEMIEUX, 13]

020

Those who would argue Mario Lemieux was the most physically and naturally talented player ever to play the game would almost certainly use the 1988-89 season as Exhibit A in their opening statement.

That was the year Lemieux set the record for shorthanded goals in a season with 13. But what many people don't realize is that Lemieux also scored 31 power play goals, which gave him the most combined shorthanded and power play markers in a season ever.

That Lemieux was that dangerous on both sides of the man advantage that season was remarkable. In that era, the penalty-killing duties were largely covered by the checking forwards, but Penguins coach Gene Ubriaco obviously knew Lemieux could be dangerous in any situation and decided to use him in that role. It also helped that Lemieux had ample opportunity to display his penalty-killing prowess since the Penguins averaged 33.2 penalty minutes per game that season, which is second-highest in league history.

One of the things that made Lemieux such a great penalty-killer was his command of the puck and the play. Perhaps more than any player in the history of the game, Lemieux was able to hang onto the puck and fight through all kinds of checks.

Lemieux finished that season with a career-high 85 goals and 199 points, which was 31 points ahead of Wayne Gretzky. But it wasn't enough to usurp Gretzky for the Hart Trophy that season. When asked at the NHL awards ceremony whether he thought it made sense that he was the first-team all-star center ahead of Gretzky and not the Hart Trophy winner, Lemieux replied, "Nothing in this league makes sense."

021

CONSECUTIVE GAMES WITH A POINT IN ONE PLAYOFF
[BRYAN TROTTIER, 18]

From 1980 to 1984, the New York Islanders won four consecutive Stanley Cups and made a fifth appearance in the Cup final. In all they won a record 19-straight playoff series, the longest streak in the history of pro sports (one more than the NBA's Boston Celtics had from 1959 to 1967).

"We felt we could beat anyone – that's the attitude you develop as a team on a streak like that," said Mike Bossy, statistically the game's greatest ever sniper. "With the quality of players we had – Bryan Trottier, Denis Potvin, Billy Smith – it seemed there was always someone there to do the heavy lifting if another of us wasn't at his best."

In dissecting the streak, the heavy lifting Hall of Fame center Trottier in particular managed can't be overlooked. He elevated his game during the dynasty years and in the 1981 post-season tournament, set a record by producing at least one point in 18 consecutive games (Wayne Gretzky and Al MacInnis came closest to breaking it with 17-game runs; Gretzky in 1988, MacInnis in '89).

"We felt we could beat anyone – that's the attitude you develop as a team on a streak like that."

Mike Bossy

More impressively, from the period of 1980 to 1982, Trottier had points in 27 straight playoff games – a mark that has even less chance of being broken than his mark of 18 games in a single playoff. Again, Gretzky was the one to come closest to matching Trottier's consistency, but the margin of difference

Bryan Trottier

was even greater, as 'The Great One' could manage only (and we use "only" in the loosest sense of the word) 19 games spanning two post-seasons.

When you consider Trottier accumulated 42 points during the 27-game streak, it is clear he wasn't making lemonade from lemons. He was exceptional even in a league of outstanding players because he was surrounded by cream-of-the-crop talent. That's why Bossy is quick to credit his teammates when discussing his numerous NHL records – and why he believes Trottier or any other player would need a degree of help to reach the collective and individual heights they reached.

"We made each other better players," Bossy said of Trottier. "He was an amazing talent to begin with, but we challenged each other to push ourselves to the limit." ▌Adam Proteau

---

022

SHORTHANDED GOALS IN ONE GAME
[THEOREN FLEURY, 3]

I t happened more than 20 years ago, but among Theo Fleury's other talents is the memory of an elephant. Just about all the details of one remarkable night - an NHL record three shorthanded goals against a very good St. Louis Blues team on March 9, 1991 - are firmly etched in his mind.

He remembers exactly how each goal played out. How they were the 44th, 45th and 46th goals of the one and only year in which he scored 50. How playing the year, on right wing, with Doug Gilmour for the first time, made life easier as a goal-scorer. And above all, he remembers how that night rivaled the game he went plus-9 in a rout of the 1992-93 San Jose Sharks as the most memorable regular season achievement in his 1,084-game NHL career.

Fleury's record-setting night took place in his third NHL season, only two years after the Flames won the 1989 Stanley Cup. The team was still an NHL power with championship potential.

Theoren Fleury
may have played
for other teams,
but he will
always be a
Flame at heart.

"We were good then, but they were good, too," said Fleury of the Blues. "They had Scott Stevens on the point. They had Adam Oates and Brett Hull, too. I remember Vinny Riendeau was the goalie and on the last goal he didn't even try. He left his legs wide open because he was so pissed off I already had two shorthanded goals before that.

"It was me and Steph Matteau on the first goal. He stole the puck in the zone and he threw it across to me and I one-timed it in the net. On the other two, I just stole the puck and went in on a breakaway. Adam Oates, he skates like a turtle, so..."

No, Oates was good at a lot of other things, but foot speed was never his strong suit and Fleury, at that point, had exceptional acceleration and breakaway speed.

"It was one of those nights when you feel good," said Fleury. "And back then, you have Brett Hull on one team and our team was pretty offensive, too. There wasn't a whole lot of trapping going on."

> *"It was one of those crazy years for me when everything I shot went in the net. I had five hat tricks that year."*
> Theo Fleury

It was also Doug Risebrough's first year as coach, after he replaced Terry Crisp. In his playing days, Risebrough was known as a premier penalty killer and the Flames were a threat that year shorthanded.

"It was one of those crazy years for me when everything I shot went in the net," said Fleury, who received a lot of ice time on the penalty kill. "I had five hat tricks that year. When you get on a roll and have confidence and play with great players, which I was doing at that time, it's pretty easy to get points and goals."

Many thought early on the 5-foot-6 Fleury would top out as a minor-pro star, but Fleury broke in midway through the

1988-89 season and was in the lineup as a support/energy player when the team won its one and only Stanley Cup. In the following years, he gradually moved up the depth chart as the Flames slowly took apart their championship team. In successive years, they lost both Hakan Loob and Joe Mullen, creating room at right wing on the top two lines.

"I was as shocked as anybody to be having that type of season that quickly," Fleury said of his 1990-91 campaign. "We still had Gilmour, Joel Otto and Joe Nieuwendyk as our three centers, so it was hard for me to get more ice time playing center. They came to me and said, 'would you be interested in playing right wing?' "

"I ended up playing with Dougie (in Mullen's old spot) and we had some really good chemistry."

"He left his legs wide open because he was so pissed off I already had two shorthanded goals before that."

Theo Fleury

In all, Fleury scored 830 points in his Flames' career before leaving the team in a trade with Colorado mere days after passing Al MacInnis as their all-time leading scorer (Jarome Iginla overtook him in 2009).

Two years ago, Fleury attended Flames' training camp in a comeback attempt that came closer to succeeding than most thought possible. In the end, he couldn't crack the lineup despite producing four points in four exhibition games and tallying the shootout winner in his final game in front of the home crowd.

Since making his retirement official, Fleury has made the rounds as a motivational speaker, with a particular emphasis on recounting his experiences as a victim of sexual abuse. He is also trying his hand at a singing career with a single available on iTunes and an album in the works. Another record to add to his collection. ∎ Eric Duhatschek

023

FASTEST FIVE GOALS BY ONE TEAM
[PITTSBURGH PENGUINS, 2:07]

The Pittsburgh Penguins started the third period of their Nov. 22, 1972 game against St. Louis down 4-3. The goal judge's job was far from over, though.

The Penguins scored seven goals in the final frame to take the game in a resounding 10-4 route. The most impressive showing that night wasn't the comeback itself, however, rather the record five goals Pittsburgh scored in just 2:07.

Bryan Hextall scored at the 12-minute mark of the third period to tie the game, followed by Jean Pronovost at 12:18 to take the lead. Goals by Al McDonough (13:40), Ken Schinkel (13:49) and Ron Schock (14:07) sealed the win and the record for the Pens.

024

SHORTEST PLAYER
[ROY WORTERS, 5-FOOT-3]

At 5-foot-3, goaltender Roy 'Shrimp' Worters is the shortest player of all-time, but that didn't stop him from becoming one of the greatest goalies ever, too. Worters stood tall for a man of his stature, becoming the first goalie to win the Hart Trophy, in 1929, and winning the Vezina Trophy in 1931.

Worters spent the bulk of his career with the New York Americans and was their best player for nine seasons. He brought instant credibility to a last-place team, but that didn't translate into much success. The Americans made the playoffs just twice during Worters' tenure and when they did he was left hung out to dry. In 1929, the Americans didn't score a single goal and lost a two-game, total-score quarterfinal series, despite Worters allowing just one score to the New York Rangers. Then, in 1936, the Americans scored eight goals in five post-season games, falling in the semi-finals.

The 1969 Hall of Fame inductee, who finished with 67 shutouts in 484 games, was also a tough customer. He stood up to Americans owner and notorious bootlegger Bill Dwyer to demand a yearly salary of $8,500, a stack of money almost as tall as he was.

LONGEST SERVING CAPTAIN
[STEVE YZERMAN, 20 YEARS]

025

Canada was reeling as the hockey portion of the 2002 Winter Olympics got underway. After being whipped by Sweden in the opener, Canadian coach Pat Quinn went to Mario Lemieux and Steve Yzerman and asked for their help.

"We had a bunch of guys who were really top players, but they were all players who logged a minute-and-a-half shifts in the National Hockey League," said Quinn.

Steve Yzerman's leadership skills on the ice served him well off the ice as he quickly turned around the Tampa Bay Lightning as their GM.

When Yzerman and Lemieux, the team leaders, bought into the plan, everyone else followed suit.

"They were terrific leaders," Quinn said. "They stepped right up. They shortened their shifts and picked the pace up and that's why we became a competitive team.

"That's what leadership is all about, your good guys showing the way for the rest of the team."

Canada went on to win its first gold medal in 50 years, thanks significantly to the example set by Yzerman. He put the team ahead of himself and that is the true indication of leadership.

This is not news to the Detroit Red Wings or fans of the team, who bow in reverence to Yzerman's legacy as captain of the team for an NHL-record two decades, from 1986 to 2006.

"The leadership of Stevie Yzerman, you can't say enough about that," said Detroit coach Mike Babcock, Yzerman's last NHL coach. "He was always about the team."

"His determination and his leadership on the ice was something I really appreciated."
Nicklas Lidstrom

Yzerman set an example for all to follow. He was not about bravado, never in search of a bravo.

"When I think of Steve, I think of competitiveness and intensity," said Detroit assistant GM Jim Nill, Yzerman's teammate during his early Detroit days. "The will to win. He was going to win no matter what."

Nill explained why Yzerman sought no part of festivities that recognized his personal achievements: "He never wanted to stand out from the other players. He just wanted to be one of the guys."

When coach Jacques Demers named Yzerman captain prior to the 1986-87 season, it was with a specific purpose in mind. He saw Yzerman as not only his best player, but the guy who could lead the franchise out of the Dead Wings era – in which they'd won one playoff series since 1966 – and back to prominence.

By the time Yzerman was done leading Detroit, he'd carried the Wings to three Stanley Cups and to status as the NHL's model franchise. But don't try and tell him he had anything to do with it.

"All I did was play the games," said Yzerman.

Red Wings GM Ken Holland knows it goes well beyond that.

"The reason people fell in love with Stevie is because of his class," Holland said. "The person you see on the ice is the person you see off the ice. A caring, hardworking person with a great passion for the game and for his family and friends."

The next-longest serving captain after Yzerman, currently the GM in Tampa Bay, is another famous, and well-respected, No. 19 – former Colorado star Joe Sakic. 'Burnaby Joe' spent 16 seasons as the leader of the Quebec Nordiques/Colorado Avalanche.

> *"The leadership of Stevie Yzerman, you can't say enough about that. He was always about the team."*
> Mike Babcock

"You don't see it very often where you have one player being with one team for a long time and being the captain," said Detroit defenseman Nicklas Lidstrom, who was next to wear the 'C' after Yzerman. "Steve set a great example of being a captain and being a leader for a lot of years.

"His determination and his leadership on the ice was something I really appreciated. He wasn't saying a whole lot in the locker room, but when he spoke, it mattered. He spoke at the right moments, too."

Former teammate Brendan Shanahan summed up what made Yzerman the consummate captain: "He just played the game that he thought we should all play and led by example. That's the best kind of leadership there is." ∎ Bob Duff

Big, Bad
& Steely

026

PENALTY MINUTES BY A SCORING CHAMPION
[STAN MIKITA, 154]

'Terrible' Ted Lindsay created a monster when he gave 19-year-old Stan Mikita advice back in 1959.

A four-time Cup winner with Detroit, Lindsay stood 5-foot-8, 163 pounds, yet was the toughest hombre in the NHL. Traded to Chicago late in his career, he saw something special in 5-foot-9, 165-pound rookie Mikita and passed along words of wisdom.

"If you want to last in the NHL," Lindsay told his Hawks teammate, "you must hit the other guy first."

Mikita learned quickly. Though he scored just 26 points in a checking-line capacity his first season, he racked up 119 penalty minutes, fourth most in the league.

The offense started to come in his sophomore season, but he didn't abandon his aggressive play as he moved up the depth chart. By his fifth season, Mikita led the league with 87 points and his 146 PIM (third most in the league) were the highest ever by a scoring champion, eclipsing Jean Beliveau's 143 from 1955-56.

Mikita did one better the next season, 1964-65. He repeated as winner of the Art Ross Trophy and topped his own record with 154 PIM (seventh most in the league) for a scoring champion. That record still stands today.

Then Lindsay got to Mikita again.

Lindsay appreciated the chippy, productive style Mikita displayed, but told Stan he'd need an extra long stick to score from the penalty box. Maybe Mikita listened to that and additional advice from home.

In his autobiography, *I Play To Win*, Mikita says his wife told him his daughter was watching a game on TV and asked, "Mommy, why does Daddy spend so much time sitting down?" The camera had showed Mikita in the penalty box.

From pugilistic to peaceful, Stan Mikita's career did a 180 in the mid-1960s and it earned him two Lady Byng Trophies.

The future Hall of Famer changed his ways and won the NHL scoring titles again in 1966-67 and 1967-68, this time with 12 and 14 PIM totals. Mikita also won the Lady Byng Trophy those two seasons.

PENALTY MINUTES IN ONE SEASON
[DAVE SCHULTZ, 472]

Imagine one of today's players averaging a five-minute major penalty per game.

Pretty scary, right?

Well, then, conjure up the fear factor living in the hearts of NHL competitors in the early '70s when they had to face a guy who piled up an average of that aforementioned quintet of infraction increments a night, with about 60 minutes to spare.

That was the climate in the brief, turbulent world of Dave 'The Hammer' Schultz, the Philadelphia Flyers' ultimate bad boy whose 472 penalty minutes total in 1974-75 is a record that will likely never be broken.

Schultz pretty much put the "bull" in the notorious Broad Street Bullies. He was a proactive enforcer, dropping the gloves if someone so much as looked at him cross-eyed.

Around him there were other tough guys – Andre 'Moose' Dupont, Bob 'Hound' Kelly and Ed 'Goodnight, Valeri Kharlamov' Van Impe.

But Schultz was the ringleader. He was chiefly responsible for creating the phenomenon known as "The Philly Flu," the tag hung on the urban legend of visiting players calling in sick when they arrived at the circus tent known as the Spectrum.

"He was the most intimidating player in the NHL," said former teammate Bill Clement, who had a ringside view of the daily pugilistic performances. "One of the things our team was built to do was an attempt to make sure that no one took advantage of us.

"Bobby Clarke was our captain, but the captain of our intimidation was Dave Schultz."
Bill Clement

"I think in the construction of the team, the Frankenstein monster, got a little ahead of the prototype."

No doubt. Schultz was particularly aggressive at home. Spurred on by a segment of loosely organized vocal fans calling themselves "Schultz's Army," he would get something started early and the building would begin to jump.

No wonder the Flyers were an amazing 96-14-9 at their barn between 1973 and 1976.

"Nobody in the NHL was feared as much as Dave," Clement said. "Hockey has always been at least part intimidation. And Dave was Captain Intimidator. Bobby Clarke was our captain, but the captain of our intimidation was Dave Schultz."

Perhaps the most graphic example of this premeditated mayhem came in Game 7 of the 1974 Eastern Conference final between the Flyers and New York Rangers at the Spectrum.

Early in the game, Schultz – who also holds the NHL record for most penalty minutes (42) in a playoff game – went after New York defenseman Dale Rolfe, not known for his fighting skills. It was a bloodbath, got the crowd into the game and paved the way to a 4-3 win. Two weeks later, the Flyers made history by becoming the first expansion team to win the Stanley Cup.

Of course there were critics of both Schultz's tactics and the NHL's decision to look the other way. The Flyers made little secret of the fact they had loaded their team with enforcers to counter the beatings they had taken in previous years from teams like the St. Louis Blues and the big, bad Boston Bruins.

With Schultz on board, the playground bullies ran for cover.

"I remember him fighting Denis Potvin right near the glass," Clement said. "Denis wore one of those Riddell cut-out football helmets, the kind Stan Mikita used to wear.

"Schultzie hit him so hard, the helmet ended up in the second row."

Ironically, Schultz began his hockey career as an offensive player in junior hockey, but he quickly turned to relying on his fighting prowess as a pro, first with the Salem Rebels of the Eastern League and later with the Quebec Aces and Richmond Robins of the American League.

When he arrived in Philadelphia for the 1972-73 season, coach Fred Shero made the mission clear. Schultz began building his reputation, one fight at a time.

"I remember he fought Dale Tallon in Vancouver and Tallon managed to get Dave's jersey over his head," Clement said. "Even with that, Dale ended up with a huge cut over his eye and a separated shoulder.

"I think in the construction of the team, the Frankenstein monster, got a little ahead of the prototype."
Bill Clement

"Dave knew where he was punching at all times. He would take punches to get started. He always knew how to use his left hand to hold the other player's right shoulder."

To put it all in perspective, Chicago's Keith Magnuson held the league record of 291 minutes before Schultz arrived. The closest to come to Schultz's record in the past 36 years was Pittsburgh's Paul Baxter with 409 in 1981-82.

Will anyone ever break it?

"Dan Carcillo told me he tried to break Dave's record his first year in the league (324 minutes in 57 games with Phoenix in 2007-08)," Clement chuckled. "That's how he got his nickname, 'Car Bomb.' He said he had to act like an idiot all year." ∎ Wayne Fish

POWER PLAY GOALS IN ONE SEASON
[TIM KERR, 34]

The goals came a little more often during the mid-1980s, but the guys scoring them tended to be the same humble types hockey is still littered with today.

Tim Kerr set an NHL record with 34 power play goals in 76 games for the Philadelphia Flyers in 1985-86, but cited Swedish setup artist Pelle Eklund as the real engine that drove the man advantage.

When Kerr tied the old mark of 28 power play goals originally set by Mike Bossy and Phil Esposito, Eklund had assisted on 15 of his tallies.

"I don't think there's any question he's been the difference on our power play this season," Kerr told The Hockey News that season. "I know everybody is looking at my number of goals, but all that means is that the entire power play is working better – and not just me."

Man-advantage markers – like goals in general – came more frequently in the era Kerr was filling the net for the Flyers. During the '85-86 season, the league average for power play success was more than 22 percent, as opposed to a little more than 18 percent in 2010-11. Eighteen of the 21 teams had a conversion rate of better than 20 percent in 1985-86, while 24 of 30 clubs were worse than 20 percent in 2010-11.

Kerr's Flyers had the fifth-best power play outfit in the league at slightly less than 24 percent and Michel Goulet of the Nordiques also equaled Bossy and Esposito with 28 tallies while his team was up a man that year.

Kerr also led the league in power play goals the season before and after his record-setting campaign, with 21 in 1984-85 and 26 in 1986-87. Dave Andreychuk came within two goals of tying Kerr's mark in 1992-93, when he racked up 32 power play goals playing 83 games for Buffalo and Toronto. Andreychuk holds the all-time record for career power play goals with 274. Nobody has seriously threatened Kerr's single-season standard of late.

Signed as a free agent by Philly in 1979, Kerr used his 6-foot-3, 230-pound frame to dominate the front of the net. His career was cut short by knee and shoulder injuries, but for an idea of how much of an impact he had consider he is the only Flyer with four 50-goal seasons on the books, including the 58 he totalled in both 1985-86 and 1986-87.

In all, Kerr scored 370 times in 655 career games for a 0.56 goals-per-game average. Cam Neely, who is in the Hockey Hall of Fame, scored 395 goals in 726 games, putting his goals-per-game average at 0.54, slightly less than Kerr's.

GOALS BY A PENALTY MINUTES LEADER
[TIGER WILLIAMS, 35]

029

When you think of players known for their goal celebrations, the one thing they have in common is that, naturally, they tend to be regular lamp-lighters.

Alex Ovechkin's glass slam, Danny Briere's exaggerated uppercut or even Jaromir Jagr's modified army salute from the 1990s all serve as examples of excellent players punctuating what they do best with a little fun.

Then there's Tiger Williams. The lasting image most carry with them of the NHL's all-time penalty minutes leader is likely something akin to the chokehold Homer puts on Bart during any number of *The Simpsons* episodes; just flip Tiger for Homer and Bart for some poor European player who wanted to see what North American hockey was all about during the '70s.

"Even before practice started, he would go on and shoot 150 pucks before anyone was on and 150 after."

Stan Smyl

The other enduring Tiger-related vision would be the sight of him vigorously "riding the stick" after scoring what you might assume to be a rare goal. The celebration was unique, but the goals were actually more common than most would guess.

In fact, Williams holds the record for the most goals scored in one season by a player who led the league in penalties minutes when he watched an NHL-best 343 minutes of hockey from the box and scored 35 goals in 1980-81.

As a cherry on top of that mark, Williams became only the third player in NHL history (after Maurice Richard in 1952-53 and Nels Stewart in 1926-27) to lead the league in PIM and his team, the Canucks, in goals.

Stan Smyl scored 63 points that season for Vancouver, one more than Williams' 62. He said the legendary tough guy was one of the hardest-working players on the squad.

"Even before practice started, he would go on and shoot 150 pucks before anyone was on and 150 after," said Smyl, who was third on the Canucks with 171 PIM that season.

Despite working diligently to improve his shot, most of Williams' goals were borne out of the fact he happily went where you were bound to take a few hacks and whacks before getting your stick on the puck.

"Every goal he earned that year was a battle to the front of the net," Smyl said.

In the 1990s, players such as Keith Tkachuk and Eric Lindros earned a reputation as big-time goal scorers who racked up penalty minutes, but neither came truly close to matching Williams' feat. In the Original Six era, Gordie Howe's soft hands and sharp elbows had him near the top of a few statistical categories, but he never pulled the double Williams did.

Williams was an asset to his club because of the fierce manner in which he approached the game.

These days, Corey Perry is about the best combination of goals and grit going, but the 2010-11 Rocket Richard winner isn't going to be the league's PIM king anytime soon.

Smyl said Williams was an asset to his club because the fierce manner in which he approached the game created room for both his teammates and himself. Though not a frequent linemate of Williams', when Smyl did skate beside him, he was always in the middle of the fun.

"With Tiger," he said, "you knew you were going to be involved in the game" ▌ Ryan Dixon

Dave 'Tiger' Williams had soft hands and hard knuckles. Ask any goalie or fight opponent.

030

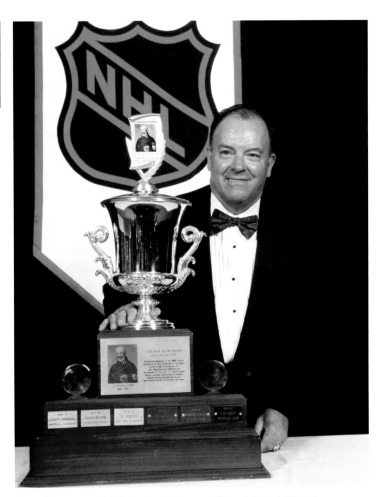

Scotty Bowman guided the Red Wings to 131 points in 1995-96 and for that claimed his second Jack Adams Award.

COACHING WINS
[SCOTTY BOWMAN, 1,244]

We're going to go out on a limb and assume Pat Quinn has coached his last NHL game, although you never know when it comes to a league whose recycling of coaches makes it a favorite with environmentalists.

But consider that even if Quinn were to somehow resurface, he'd have to coach another nine seasons and win roughly 62 games per season in order to catch Scotty Bowman in games coached (2,141) and victories (1,244).

If Bowman were not such a brilliant and innovative coach, you'd be tempted to chalk up all of his success to the fact that he found himself standing behind some of the greatest players in the history of the game. There is undoubtedly some credence to that, considering the three teams in NHL history to accumulate the most points – the 1976-77 Montreal Canadiens with 132, the 1995-96 Detroit Red Wings with 131 and the 1977-78 Canadiens with 129 – were all coached by Bowman.

But Bowman hardly just stood behind the bench chewing on ice chips. A big reason why those teams were so great – particularly the Canadiens teams of the 1970s – was that they were relentless in their approach to the game. There's no doubt they adopted the persona of their coach, who excelled by ensuring that every player from the superstar to the fourth-liner was on edge.

But Bowman's teams weren't always a collection of Hall of Fame talent. In his first three seasons as a coach in the NHL, Bowman led the expansion St. Louis Blues to two division finals and three straight Stanley Cup finals.

Top Of The Flops

FEWEST WINS BY A TEAM IN ONE SEASON
[WASHINGTON CAPITALS, 8]

031

They never had a chance.

The 1974-75 Washington Capitals began their inaugural season at the tail end of an expansion boom that saw the NHL grow from six teams to 18 and its talent base spread thin. Draconian rules in the expansion draft allowed existing franchises to keep their best players and top prospects. And the upstart World Hockey Association drained that talent pool further by luring away NHL players with the promise of better salaries.

Under those onerous conditions, Washington and the Kansas City Scouts were tasked with building competitive teams. Both had predictably terrible seasons. But no team in NHL history has finished a campaign with fewer wins or points than those 1974-75 Caps, whose 8-67-5 record and 21 points still stands as the record for futility. They ended the year with a .131 winning percentage, also the worst in league history.

"I tell people those might have been some bad times for the franchise, but they were still some of the best years of my life," said defenseman Yvon Labre, who played seven seasons in Washington and had his number retired by the organization. "I pride myself that after five years I was the only guy left from the original team. Lots of guys wanted to leave. I didn't. I wanted to see it through."

Labre and his teammates endured enough losses to last an entire career that first season. The Caps actually earned a tie on Oct. 15, 1974 against the Los Angeles Kings in their third game – the first NHL contest played at the Capital Centre in suburban Landover, Md. – and then beat the Chicago Blackhawks for their first victory two days later. But those games proved a mirage. Washington immediately hit a 0-13-1 skid before getting a win in a home game against the California Golden Seals Nov. 19. It would be almost a month before they earned another one.

The long, winless stretches were a consistent theme that year. Jimmy Anderson was fired as coach Feb. 9. His replacement, Red Sullivan, lasted 18 games before stomach ulcers and 14 consecutive losses drove him from the job. Caps GM Milt Schmidt finished out the season's final eight games behind the bench. It was Schmidt who put the team together, so it was only fair he also coached the final three games of what became an NHL record 17-game losing streak. That mark still stands today, though the 1992-93 San Jose Sharks tied it.

Washington found it virtually impossible to win away from Capital Centre. The Caps were outscored 256-83 on the road. That included a pair of 12-1 losses, at Boston and Pittsburgh, and an 11-1 beating in Montreal. Not that Washington was much better at home. The squad set another NHL record: 446 goals allowed in one season. That's 31 more than the next closest team in history, the 1985-86 Detroit Red Wings (415).

"I tell people those might have been some bad times for the franchise, but they were still some of the best years of my life."

Yvon Labre

And poor goalie Michel Belhumeur didn't win a single game all season. In fact, his two-year stint with the Caps was a complete disaster as he compiled a 0-29-4 record.

One of the few highlights of that season was finally winning a game away from home. It didn't happen until March 28 – Game 76 – but when the Caps beat the Golden Seals 5-3 at Oakland-Alameda County Coliseum, they wanted to enjoy it. Center Tommy Williams and some teammates wrapped a green garbage can with duct tape and passed it around the dressing room like their own version of a mutant Stanley Cup. They even signed their names on it to commemorate the moment.

"The hockey season is a long trek and there's a lot of kidding going on and wise cracks and laughter," long-time Washington play-by-play broadcaster Ron Weber said. "That's a built-in reaction to boredom and maybe frustration if you're a losing team. In the case of the 1974-75 Capitals, I don't think there was a real bad-apple grouch among them. Some were more universally liked than others, of course, but I think it was a good group and they were definitely resilient."

They had to be. Even the brand-new Capital Centre had its issues. Weber remembers a home game against the New York Rangers on a Tuesday night that didn't start until 10 p.m. The problem? The circus had just left town and no one bothered to clean up the elephant urine. The fresh sheet of ice couldn't stick to the concrete underneath, leaving a patchwork of holes all over the surface that needed to be repaired. It was that kind of year.

In the case of the 1974-75 Capitals, I don't think there was a real bad-apple grouch among them."

Ron Weber

There was one more dubious record, this one set by a single player. Bill Mikkelson, a 26-year-old defenseman, played 59 games that season and contributed three goals and seven assists. But he was also a minus-82, the worst number for any NHL player since the league began tracking the stat in 1968. Weber contends that in a game halfway through the season, Mikkelson was given a minus despite not being on the ice, though Weber conceded one fewer minus wouldn't have made the defenseman feel any better. Mikkelson was demoted to the American League's Richmond Robins before the end of the season and would play just one more NHL game with Washington, in 1976-77. Like many of his teammates, the expansion Caps had provided a once-in-a-lifetime chance.

"It was an opportunity for guys that might not have played for the other teams to come out and play," Labre said. "I had played on and off with Pittsburgh, but this gave me a chance to stay and play in the NHL. For that I will be eternally grateful. That's not a bad thing. That's a good thing." ∎ Brian McNally

Guy Charron came within a couple of points of making the playoffs on several occasions, but the breaks never went his way.

GAMES PLAYED WITHOUT MAKING THE PLAYOFFS
[GUY CHARRON, 734]

032

There are two cruel things about Guy Charron's claim to fame in the record book.

The first is that he was a quality player who had four 70-point seasons, but somehow was unlucky enough to play his entire 734-game career without making it to the playoffs.

The second – and most sadistic – is Charron is destined to experience setting the record over and over again, as though he is Bill Murray in *Groundhog Day*. That's because whenever a playoff-challenged NHLer surpasses Charron's career game total, that player is bound to make the post-season down the road, thereby putting that dubious distinction back in Charron's possession.

The most sadistic cruelty is Charron is destined to experience setting the record over and over again.

Such was the case in 2008-09 when Olli Jokinen surpassed Charron's 734 games and bumped the record-setting total to 799 games. Problem was Jokinen's Calgary Flames made the playoffs that season and the big Finn was no longer a post-season virgin.

Back to you, Guy.

Move forward two seasons later and Calgary's Jay Bouwmeester has reached the 635-game mark without making the playoffs. If the rebuilding Flames don't reach the post-season in 2011-12 and Bouwmeester doesn't miss any time, Charron's mark will fall early in 2012-13.

What's shocking about Charron's record is making the post-season was easier than it is today when just 16 of 30 teams make it. He played a couple seasons when 16 of 21 teams made the spring run.

Charron's teams missed the playoffs by an average 18 points per season. He spent his first four seasons with a rebuilding team in Detroit, then seven years with expansion teams (two with Kansas City and five with Washington).

His Wings missed the playoffs once by two points. The Capitals were reaching respectability at the end of Charron's career, but missed the playoffs by two points in 1979-80 and one point in 1980-81, Charron's final NHL season. Washington made the playoffs the very next year.

FEWEST GOALS BY A TEAM IN ONE PLAYOFF SERIES (BEST-OF-SEVEN)
[MINNESOTA WILD, 1]

The Minnesota Wild entered the 2003 Western Conference final against the Mighty Ducks of Anaheim with 42 goals during the playoffs, 12 more than any other team still playing. Having already come back from 3-1 series deficits twice to upset the Colorado Avalanche and Vancouver Canucks, the Wild, only in their third season and led by young sniper Marian Gaborik, were looking to complete an improbable run to the Stanley Cup final.

But to say their offense ran dry would be an understatement. After failing to find the net for three games, Minnesota finally broke through on its fourth shot of Game 4, when Andrew Brunette beat J-S Giguere 4:37 into the first period for the only Wild goal of the series. Giguere, who won the Conn Smythe Trophy that year, had stopped the first 101 shots Minnesota directed his way and finished the series with an amazing .992 save percentage as the Ducks swept their way to the final.

It marked the first time a team had been held to just one goal during a series since 1976, when the Los Angeles Kings smothered the Atlanta Flames in their best-of-three opening-round set.

UNDRAFTED PLAYERS USED IN ONE SEASON (18-SKATER LINEUPS)
[NEW YORK ISLANDERS, 14]

I t began, like so many other recent stories surrounding the New York Islanders, with Rick DiPietro. The brash goal-tender with the 15-year mega-contract played just five games for the Isles in 2008-09, facilitating the need for a backup. Or, as the case turned out to be, several backups.

DiPietro's knee injury ruined his campaign, but the fact is no Islander went the distance that season - defenseman Mark Streit topped the charts with 74 games played. The result was a lot of call-ups (43 total players used, with 11 suiting up for less than 10 contests each) and the unusual grand total of 14 undrafted men playing at least one game – a modern-day record since game-night rosters were expanded to 18 skaters and two goalies in 1982-83.

Just how peculiar is it to use that many undrafted players? Consider that in the 10 seasons between 1999 and 2010 just seven out of 298 squads have iced double digits, with the second highest being the 2002-03 Atlanta Thrashers with 11.

Midway through the 2008-09 season, New York was dead last in the NHL with a 12-29-5 record and boasting a goaltending duo of Joey MacDonald and Yann Danis – both undrafted free agents. Another free agent netminder, Peter Mannino, made his NHL debut that season and was promptly shelled. His 4.51 goals-against average was the worst of the lot, but on the bright side, his 1-1-0 record in three appearances gave him the only non-losing record on the team. Mannino played two games for the Atlanta Thrashers in 2010-11, so his NHL career still has light. Some of the other undrafted recruits would kill for two more NHL games.

Not a bad fate for a player who attended Norwich College and once played in the old United League for the Richmond Riverdogs.

Jamie Fraser, a defenseman who played one game in '08-09, has split time between the American League and ECHL, while Sean Bentivoglio was last seen plying his trade in Germany. Kurtis McLean did a four-game tour of duty for the Isles that year and is now a solid player for Lukko Rauma in Finland. Not a bad fate, in fact, for a player who attended Norwich College and once played in the old United League for the Richmond Riverdogs.

But if any good game out of that losing season, it was the fact that the Islanders were so bad, they ended up with the No. 1 pick in the draft. Their prize? Center John Tavares.

LOSSES BY A TEAM IN ONE SEASON
[SAN JOSE SHARKS, 71]

035

The 1992-93 season saw two expansion teams go toe-to-toe for the all-time futility mark with the San Jose Sharks edging out the Ottawa Senators by one loss. Only the Senators scored fewer goals than the 'Floundering Fins' and no team allowed more, as San Jose played to an 11-71-2 record in what would be George Kingston's second and last season as an NHL bench boss.

A lineup of cast-aside veterans and untested youngsters combined to make a team that was ineffective on offense and porous on defense. Kelly Kisio (78 points) and Johan Garpenlov (66) led the attack, but after that pair no Shark hit the 45-point plateau. Not a single skater's plus-minus was better than minus-1 and defensemen Doug Zmolek, Rob Zettler and Neil Wilkinson all tied for a team-worst minus-50.

Four goalies were left to face 36.6 shots per game and only one finished with a goals-against average below 5.00 (Arturs Irbe, 4.11). Jeff Hackett won two games in 36 appearances.

Looking back, this disastrous season only makes the Sharks' upset over top-seeded Detroit during the first round of the playoffs the following year even more impressive.

Early on the Sharks fought a good fight, but rarely found the 'W' column.

Stephen Weiss broke into the NHL in 2001-02 and has witnessed nine of the record 10 playoff-less campaigns in Florida.

CONSECUTIVE SEASONS MISSING THE PLAYOFFS
[FLORIDA PANTHERS, 10]

036

Even though the Florida Panthers were swept in the opening round of the 2000 playoffs, there was plenty of optimism surrounding the team the following year.

The 1999-2000 season had been Florida's best ever (43 wins) and the Cats boasted a 58-goal Rocket Richard winner and Hart Trophy candidate in Pavel Bure. In June, Florida also pulled a blockbuster trade to land high-end youngsters Olli Jokinen and Roberto Luongo. Spirits were high.

"It seems there's an attitude that we know we're a good team now," captain and original Panther Scott Mellanby told THN during training camp in 2000.

Despite another 59 goals from Pavel Bure and an outstanding season from Roberto Luongo, Florida went from 98 points to 66.

But instead of getting better, the wheels came off and Florida began a record streak of 10 consecutive playoff-less campaigns.

Despite another Richard-winning 59 goals from Bure and an outstanding rookie season from goalie Luongo, Florida went from 98 points to 66. The Murrays, GM Bryan and coach Terry, were both canned before January. And heart-and-soul Mellanby was moved in February along with veterans Mike Sillinger and Ray Whitney. The seemingly never-ending rebuild had begun.

Instead of taking one step back in favor of two steps forward, Florida began a string of four straight miserable seasons that ended with them drafting no worse than seventh in the first round.

Stephen Weiss, Nathan Horton, Jay Bouwmeester and Rostislav Olesz were once considered the base of a promising future that never did transpire. Now, Jacob Markstrom, Dmitry Kulikov, Erik Gudbranson and others are considered the future for Panthers fans, who, for good reason, are a more cynical group now than in the '90s.

Florida's record run eclipsed the once-miserable Colorado Rockies/New Jersey Devils dry spell (1979 to 1987), which is ironic considering the last time Florida was in the playoffs their season was ended thanks to a sweep at the hands of New Jersey.

SMALLEST CROWD

037

[NEW JERSEY DEVILS, 334]

When you think of sparse attendance figures for an NHL game, you picture a bad night in Atlanta or Phoenix – a few thousand fans spread out across a sea of empty seats. But how hollow must it have felt in New Jersey on the night of Jan. 22, 1987, when a mere 334 fans were in the stands?

Of course, the low attendance that evening had nothing to do with the teams and everything to do with the weather. A vicious snowstorm that pounded the Eastern Seaboard from Georgia to New York took a toll on New Jersey's roads.

"Traditionally players take a nap around 1:00 or 1:30 and there wasn't a snowflake in sight," said Doug Sulliman, a member of that Devils squad. "I woke up around 3:30 to have a cup of tea and there had to be two feet of snow on the g   . it was still coming."

Sulliman was lucky in that he didn't liv   a the rink, though his trip tells you everything yo·   , know about how difficult it was to get around tha'   Since he had a Jeep Wrangler, Sulliman wasn't c   about the road conditions. But what he wasn't cour   ere the number of abandoned cars littering the stree'   ructing his path.

> "I woke up arour   ） to have a cup of
> tea and there h/   ے two feet of snow
> on the ground ﹏   was still coming."
>
> Doug Sulliman

"I couldn't get on the regular westbound highway," Sulliman explained. "So what I did was get on the off-ramp and backed up on the eastbound side and I drove in reverse for three miles weaving in and out of parked cars all the way to the rink."

Sulliman was one of the first to get there, but there were so many late arrivals that the game's 7:30 start time was pushed back to 9:22.

"The referee kept saying 'when you have 14 players we're starting' and we just kept hiding guys who were coming in," Sulliman said. "We didn't want to start the game until we had everyone."

Ironically, it was the road team that had little trouble getting to the rink on time. The Flames were staying across the road from Brendan Byrne Arena and were all ready to go. As they waited, both teams took two or three warmups, with the Devils shooting around with about six skaters.

What's amazing is that any fans showed up at all.

"I think the only people in the stands were trying to find solace from the storm," Sulliman said.

The game lacked intensity overall, though it did ramp up towards the end as New Jersey held a one-goal lead until an empty-netter secured a 7-5 victory. It was a strange evening to have a career game, but Sulliman exploded with a tremendously productive three periods.

"Of course, I had a career night, three goals and two assists, and nobody knew it," Sulliman laughed. "It was hilarious. It was beautiful."

"It was hilarious. It was beautiful."
Doug Sulliman

While concession workers had little to do and spent most of their time watching the game from the aisles, Sulliman remembers something coming from the stands. Normally, voices of yelling fans are lost in a large crowd, but there was one fan each player noticed during this specific tilt.

"There was this one guy who had something to say about everything on both teams," Sulliman recalled. "We had this one big mouth in the corner – I don't know if he had about six beers in him or what – but he was having the time of his life just cutting everybody up. Then we were all kind of joking that maybe one of us could catch him – you know, just step aside and I'll whistle one up over the glass at him."

The Devils public relations staff went around to each of the spectators in the building that night to gather their contact information. They later received a pin, t-shirt and got tickets to the next Devils-Flames game or the closest contest to the one-year anniversary. They were also invited to a game and private reception during the team's 25th anniversary season.

Not a bad haul for the fans who will forever be members of the very exclusive "334 Club." ▌Rory Boylen

Working Overtime

038

CONSECUTIVE OVERTIME WINS BY A GOALIE IN THE PLAYOFFS
[PATRICK ROY, 10]

Surrounded by the four walls of his small office at the Montreal Forum, coach Jacques Demers felt under siege. Three nights earlier, his Montreal Canadiens had opened the 1993 playoffs on the road against their provincial rival, the Quebec Nordiques. After two losses, the stunned Habs were in a hole.

Outside the Forum, the pouring rain matched the gloom that had suddenly engulfed Montreal. For Demers and the players there was no escaping the Canadiens' dire predicament. On radio, hosts and callers vented; in print, writers and readers raged; and the television mercilessly replayed it all over and over again.

> *"I don't think that record will ever be broken."*
> Jacques Demers

Stepping into Demers' office that morning was the one man enduring the brunt of the blame. Patrick Roy was undoubtedly the Habs' biggest star and was recognized as one of the sport's top goaltenders. But it had been seven long years since he had held the Stanley Cup aloft and fans were growing increasingly impatient. A subpar performance the night before in Montreal's 4-1 loss only served to heighten the criticism directed at the beleaguered netminder. Adding salt to the wound were the very public comments that same day by Daniel Bouchard, the former Nordiques goalie and the current Quebec goaltending coach. At one time Bouchard had been the goaltender that

Roy idolized above all others. Now he proudly claimed that Quebec had located the Montreal goaltender's "weak spot."

Outside the Forum many were calling for Roy to take his leave from the Montreal net. Inside the Forum there was never any doubt.

"I never hesitated to stick with Patrick," Demers said.

Against the backdrop of sudden death, Roy turned aside all 65 shots directed his way.

The conversation that morning between the two men was both short and to the point. In a forceful manner at the season's most crucial moment, Demers informed Roy that he was "going with him no matter what" emphasizing that he would "live or die with (him)."

"I knew that I was dealing with a winner, a competitor," Demers said. "Patrick Roy is an emotional human being. All the stuff being written in the newspapers, the stuff being said on the radio, he knew it all. No doubt it affected him. At that particular time he needed the support of his head coach and my support was unconditional. As for the rest of the team, they always believed in him."

It's during such moments that Stanley Cup history made. The Patrick Roy who had entered Demers' office mere minutes before now emerged a changed man. What followed the next six weeks was a run of playoff goaltending for the ages.

Following that crucial meeting, the Habs became an unstoppable, if improbable, force. Led by a determined and rejuvenated Roy, Montreal's journey to a most unexpected Cup began the next night. Four consecutive wins versus the Nordiques, a subsequent sweep of the Sabres and back-to-back five-game conquests of the Islanders and Kings equaled 16 wins in 18 post-season contests – and an unprecedented 24th Stanley Cup.

Included in that was a record performance by Roy, 10 consecutive overtime victories, a mark that stands nearly two decades later.

"I don't think that record will ever be broken," said Demers, who now proudly occupies a seat in the Canadian Senate.

And while seven different players scored the goals that ended the 10 overtimes – a testament to how much of a balanced team the 1993 Canadiens were – it was Roy who stood above all others.

He manned the Montreal goal for all of the 96 minutes and 39 seconds of overtime that spring. Against the backdrop of sudden death, facing the most intense pressure hockey has to offer, he turned aside all 65 shots directed his way. At the conclusion of the playoffs he was rewarded with his second Conn Smythe Trophy. In the process Roy firmly established himself as one of the greatest clutch goalies in hockey history.

"It takes 25 guys to win a Cup and we had a lot of great players, a lot of great leaders," Demers said, "but the fact that I'm wearing a Stanley Cup ring starts with Patrick Roy."
▌ Todd Denault

OVERTIME GAMES IN ONE PLAYOFF SERIES
[MONTREAL CANADIENS VS. TORONTO MAPLE LEAFS, 5]

I n the playoffs, overtime can turn a normal player into a hero and a hero into a legend. In the 1951 Stanley Cup final, every game between the Montreal Canadiens and the Toronto Maple Leafs a produced hero and in the end, produced a legend. In the process the two clubs set the record for the most OT games in one series.

Bill Barilko's overtime Stanley Cup-winning goal is famous for its drama and his later demise.

In Game 1, the Leafs prevailed on a goal by Sid Smith. The Habs rallied back in Game 2 with an overtime winner from Maurice 'Rocket' Richard, who beat goaltender Turk Broda to a loose puck and slid it into the empty cage. When the series shifted back to Montreal, the Leafs heroics continued, with 'Teeder' Kennedy and Harry Watson scoring the winners in the third and fourth contests.

Back in Toronto and down 2-1 with less than a minute to play, the Buds pulled their goalie and Tod Sloan scored with 32 seconds left to send the game to yet another overtime session. For the fifth time in the series, the extra period ended in less than six minutes as Bill Barilko blasted a slapshot past Canadiens goalie Gerry McNeil 2:53 into overtime.

Barilko's goal lives on famously as his last. The skilled 24-year-old defenseman tragically died that summer in a plane accident near Cochrane, Ont. His body wasn't found for another 11 years, which was how long it took the Leafs to win another Stanley Cup.

His No. 5 is one of only two numbers officially retired by the Leafs.

040

FASTEST REGULAR SEASON OVERTIME GOAL
[ALEX OVECHKIN,
6 SECONDS]

On the way to setting the mark for the shortest overtime in history, Alex Ovechkin ran roughshod over Atlanta, recording a hat trick in the 3-2 victory Dec. 15, 2006. Two tallies in regulation had onlookers impressed, but the ultimate jaw-drop for Thrashers fans was how long it took Ovechkin to end the game.

Several spectators were still in the arena concourse when 'Ovie' stripped Niclas Havelid off the opening draw and buried his trademark wrist shot glove side past goalie Kari Lehtonen, a mere six seconds into the extra frame.

The goal was one of eight game-winners for Ovechkin that season and one of 52 in his first six years in the league (Jaromir Jagr is No. 1 all-time with 112).

LONGEST GAME [DETROIT RED WINGS VS. MONTREAL MAROONS, 176:30]

041

When budding hockey star Modere 'Mud' Bruneteau was working as a grains commission clerk at the Norris Grain Factory in Winnipeg during the summer of 1934, he'd often pause to admire the photo of the 1933-34 Detroit Red Wings that hung in the office of secretary C.E. Babbitt.

"I want to play for the Red Wings," Bruneteau would frequently say.

Not only would he fulfill that dream, Bruneteau would go on to score the most famous goal in franchise history, perhaps even the most famous goal in Stanley Cup lore.

From St. Boniface, Man., Bruneteau, 21, was a rookie right winger with Detroit during the 1935-36 season as the club began the Stanley Cup playoffs at the Montreal Forum against the Maroons. One hundred and 76 minutes and 30 seconds into the game, Bruneteau finally ended what today remains the longest game in Stanley Cup history.

A doggedly fought defensive struggle that ended 1-0 in Detroit's favor shattered the mark of 164:46 set by Toronto and Boston in 1933. Since that day, no Stanley Cup playoff game has come within 24 minutes of equaling this endurance mark.

There were 9,500 packed into the Forum when the puck dropped and most were still occupying their seats at 2:25 a.m. when Bruneteau tallied. Detroit goalie Normie Smith, making his Stanley Cup debut, blocked 92 shots for the shutout. Maroons netminder Lorne Chabot, who'd been on the winning side with Toronto in the previous longest game, made 67 saves in defeat.

"Bruneteau scored just about the time the milkman was starting to steam out on his morning rounds," wrote Baz O'Meara in the Montreal *Star*.

The winner came when Bruneteau joined Hec Kilrea on a two-man rush toward the Montreal goal. Kilrea flipped a pass to Bruneteau, who dodged the sprawling Chabot and slipped a rolling puck into the net.

There were 9,500 packed into the Forum when the puck dropped and most were still occupying their seats at 2:25 a.m.

"It was the funniest thing," Bruneteau recalled in the book *History of Hockeytown*. "The puck just stuck there in the twine and didn't fall to the ice."

Alex Bell, a writer for *The Canadian Press*, dubbed it, "the million dollar goal."

In a 2002 interview, Red Wings right winger Pete Kelly recounted the play: "You know, to this day, that goal judge still hasn't turned on the red light."

Wound up after the long night's work, Smith headed to a Montreal establishment. "I went to a pub and had a couple beers," he told author Brian McFarlane in his book *Legendary Stanley Cup Stories*. "Then I staggered and almost fell down. People thought I was drunk, but I was simply too exhausted to stand up."

"People thought I was drunk, but I was simply too exhausted to stand up."
- Normie Smith

Not everyone was in awe of the historic moment. Ottawa *Citizen* writer Tommy Shields wondered whether the two teams would live to regret their marathon effort. He noted that Toronto had nothing left in the tank for the New York Rangers in the 1933 final after eliminating Boston in the endurance test in which those two teams engaged.

"A new overtime record for professional hockey has been set and it now remains to be seen whether or not it will produce any result other than the establishing of a mark that means nothing except as something out of the ordinary," Shields wrote. "Gruelling games of that kind cannot do otherwise than wear down the teams and individuals concerned."

This time, the overtime tilt only fired up the Wings, who swept Montreal and then downed Toronto to win their first Stanley Cup in franchise history.

At least one participant in the game, even in defeat, immediately recognized its historical significance. In the wee hours of the morning, Chabot showed up at the Montreal hotel where the Wings were lodged. Spying Detroit coach Jack Adams in the lobby, Chabot asked, "Is young Bruneteau around?" Told he was not, Chabot reached into his pocket, pulled out a puck and handed it to Adams.

"Give this to the kid," Chabot said. "It's the puck he shot past me for the winning goal. Thought he'd like to have it." ∎ **Bob Duff**

OVERTIME GOALS
[SERGEI FEDOROV, MATS SUNDIN, JAROMIR JAGR AND PATRIK ELIAS, 15]

042

According to the numbers, the most clutch players in NHL history are European. That's what one can deduce from looking at the all-time leaders when it comes to overtime goals in the regular season.

Russian Sergei Fedorov, Swede Mats Sundin and Czechs Jaromir Jagr and Patrik Elias all lead the way with 15 extra-time tallies. The NHL implemented a five-minute overtime to help settle games in 1983-84, so to be fair to Gordie Howe and the like, they never had a crack at flexing their crunch-time muscle until the playoffs. And in 1999-2000, the NHL adopted 4-on-4 overtime.

Barring an unforeseen comeback, Jagr, Sundin and Fedorov won't be padding their totals, but Elias, at 35, has a chance to establish himself as the regular season's premier extra-time player.

"I like to be in that position when the game is on the line," Elias told the New York *Post* after tying the record Dec. 4, 2008, when it was held by Sundin and Jagr.

Fedorov joined the trio when he got his 15th OT marker in his final NHL season while with the Washington Capitals March 11, 2009. The slick Russian left the NHL with 31 overtime points, the all-time record, but Elias recorded four assists in 2010-11 to pull even.

◄ Mats Sundin had a flair for the dramatic during his 18-year NHL career with the Nordiques, Maple Leafs and Canucks.

Tiny Thompson

043

SAVES IN ONE GAME
[TINY THOMPSON, 113]

He'll forever be known as 'Tiny,' but the only thing wee about Cecil Thompson was his 2.08 career goals-against average.

Hung with the wryly diminutive nickname because at 5-foot-10 he was the tallest player on one of his youth teams, Thompson came up big from the moment he entered the NHL in 1928-29, recording the first of his career 81 shutouts in his debut – the only Hall of Fame netminder ever to manage the accomplishment. That same season, he helped steer the Boston Bruins to the Stanley Cup and went on to win four Vezina Trophies in eight years – a record until Bill Durnan picked up his fifth in 1949.

Thompson also was a pioneer of sorts, a decent puckhandling goalie who became the first stopper to be credited with passing the puck for an assist and one of the first to occasionally catch pucks instead of always blocking or deflecting them. He's also documented as the first 'tender to ever be pulled in favor of an extra attacker when Art Ross called him to the bench in a 1931 contest.

His most amazing single-game feat, however, came in a playoff match defeat. On April 3 and 4, 1933 in Toronto, in the fifth and deciding game of a series, he dueled Maple Leafs goalie Lorne Chabot to a scoreless tie for more than 160 minutes. Finally, at 4:46 of the sixth overtime, Ken Dorarty beat Thompson on Toronto's 114th shot of the night to end the longest game in NHL history to that point.

A weary Thompson received a standing ovation from a pro-Leafs crowd aware they'd witnessed something special. More than 75 years later, the 113 saves Thompson recorded that night never has been bettered.

OVERTIME GOALS IN ONE PLAYOFF SERIES
[MEL HILL, 3]

044

For Mel Hill in 1939, it was all about location, location, location.

A self-described "unspectacular" player, Hill was coming off a 10-goal performance for Boston in his first full NHL regular season when he got white-hot in the first round of the playoffs against the New York Rangers. The young right winger scored three overtime goals in the series, in Games 1, 2 and 7, to propel the Bruins to the Stanley Cup final. Two of the three scores were in triple OT and none may have happened without wonderful setups from the greatest playmaker of the era, Hall of Fame center Bill Cowley.

Hill, a native of Glenboro, Man., collected three more goals in a five-game Cup triumph over Toronto, cementing his reputation as a big-game player. But it was his record-setting extra time heroics for which he'll always be remembered, goals that earned him the immortal nickname 'Sudden Death' Hill.

Chasing Stan

PLAYOFF WINS
[PATRICK ROY, 151]

045

Certainly Patrick Roy's total of 151 career playoff victories is padded by four Stanley Cup triumphs, two with Montreal and two with Colorado, but the reason he was able to distance himself from the field was the fact even his bad playoff years were pretty good.

In an 18-season career, Roy's teams failed to make the playoffs just once, when the Habs missed during the lockout-shortened 1994-95. In 17 trips to the post-season, Roy's teams advanced to the second round a staggering 14 times.

By contrast, Martin Brodeur is a distant second on the all-time list with 99 wins because his playoff career has been more boom and bust. Roy has 76 wins on the strength of four Cups, plus an additional trip to the final. Brodeur, with three championships and one loss in the final to Roy and the Avs in 2001, has 63 Ws, putting him at least in the ballpark.

But on top of those times Roy was playing for one of the final two teams, he has four more playoff seasons in which he posted double-digit victory totals.

Brodeur's Devils have missed the playoffs twice in his career and been bounced in the first round seven times.

In 17 trips to the post-season, Roy's teams advanced to the second round a staggering 14 times.

Roy played on his share of quality teams, especially the Avs outfits led by Peter Forsberg and Joe Sakic. However, the fact he posted a goals-against average below 2.00 during three deep playoff runs and a save percentage above .930 on three occasions as well speaks volumes about his crunch-time contributions, as do his three Conn Smythe Trophies, more than any player in NHL history.

046

GAME-WINNING GOALS
IN ONE PLAYOFF
[BRAD RICHARDS, 7]

A sk a Tampa Bay Lightning fan to recall the most memorable game-winning goals from the club's run to the 2004 Stanley Cup and there's a chance Brad Richards' name wouldn't come up.

That's because, despite the fact Richards set an NHL record with seven game-deciding tallies that post-season, Tampa got two goals at the tail end of that run that will forever be burned in the minds of Bolts supporters. The first was Martin St-Louis' double-overtime marker in Game 6 of the Cup final versus the Calgary Flames, which forced Game 7 in which Ruslan Fedotenko popped a pair, including the second-period winner, in a 2-1 Cup-clinching victory.

But Richards, who claimed the Conn Smythe Trophy that spring, had his fingers all over those games, too. Game 6 reached overtime because Richards scored two goals in regulation, allowing Tampa to be tied 2-2. Then, setting the tone in Game 7, he drew the first assist on Fedotenko's first-period ice-breaker.

Richards, who turned 24 just before the Eastern Conference final in 2004, kept getting better as the playoffs went on, scoring three winners through the first two rounds and four in the final two. His biggest goal in the early stages came when he tallied in overtime to put Tampa up 3-0 versus Montreal in a second-round series that ended with a sweep.

Richards' seventh winning goal came in his team's 1-0 victory over Calgary in Game 4 of the final, squaring the series 2-2. That eclipsed the six game-winners scored by Joe Sakic in 1996 and Joe Nieuwendyk in 1999. Richards led the '04 playoffs in scoring with 26 points in 23 games.

▶ Brad Richards' performance in the 2004
playoffs earned him MVP honors and put his
name in the record books.

047

GOALS BY A ROOKIE
IN THE PLAYOFFS
[DINO CICCARELLI, 14]

mprobability was the theme for the Minnesota North Stars in the 1981 playoffs. The team upset the Boston Bruins, Buffalo Sabres and Calgary Flames, before finally falling to the New York Islanders in the final.

A big reason for the remarkable run was freshman Dino Ciccarelli. After an impressive 32-game stint in the regular season, where he scored 18 goals and averaged nearly a point per game, Ciccarelli exploded for 14 tallies in the post-season, setting the rookie record.

What makes this feat, and his Hall of Fame career, even more amazing is that he was undrafted. Ciccarelli went on to amass 608 goals and is widely regarded as one of the best players never to win a Stanley Cup.

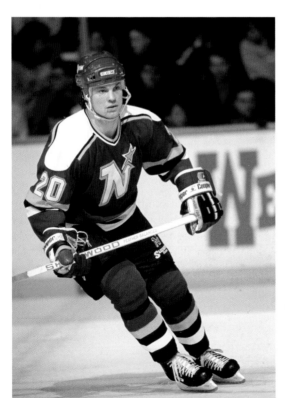

Dino Ciccarelli

CONSECUTIVE PLAYOFF SERIES WINS
[NEW YORK ISLANDERS, **19**]

048

The New York Islanders owned the playoffs like no other team in NHL history.

From 1980 to 1984, the Isles won a record 19 consecutive playoff series en route to four straight Stanley Cups and a fifth final. With parity the *cause du jour* in the NHL these days, that's a record that will never be broken.

"I think we were a machine at that point," said Denis Potvin. "We were so grooved and so emotionally sharp. It was just such a joy to play. Everything was automatic."

Islanders GM Bill Torrey's shrewd management brought a succession of star players to the bedroom community of Long Island, then the ugly stepsister of New York hockey. In five years, Torrey claimed Billy Smith in the expansion draft and nabbed Potvin, Clarke Gillies, Bryan Trottier and Mike Bossy in the draft. They were coached by Al Arbour, who had gone straight from the NHL ice to an NHL bench with St. Louis in 1970.

"We were a machine at that point."
Denis Potvin

In that group was the league's greatest ever sniper, a three-time Norris Trophy winner, an Art Ross and Hart Trophy winner who is considered one of the best two-way players in history, a Vezina Trophy-winning goaltender with a legendary mean streak and one of the league's original power forwards. Torrey and Arbour were no slouches, either, one of the best coach-GM combos the league has ever known. Seven Hall of Famers in all.

The supporting cast included John Tonelli, a playmaker with jam who could score; Butch Goring, the 1981 Conn Smythe Trophy winner; salt-of-the-earth types Brent and Duane Sutter; and the Bobs, Nystrom and Bourne, 20- to 30-goal men in their own rights. (On March 10, 1980, Torrey essentially created the frenzy that is the trade deadline by acquiring Goring. In NHL lore, he's become the mythological archetype for deadline day deals; the spark that spurred a record run.)

It all added up to a juggernaut. The Islanders finished first overall twice in those five seasons and totalled more cumulative points than any other team. On offense, the Islanders were devastating with a power play that hummed and a sixth sense of where each other would be on the ice. Defensively, they pursued the puck with a doggedness few other teams had during the go-go 1980s.

"I never had to look up and say 'Where am I moving the puck,'" Potvin said of the offense. "All those things were boom-boom, automatic."

And of the team defense: "All of those things you talk about today: the gap between defense and forward, the work down low in our own zone. We were stifling."

> ## "How many NHLers in history have played 120 playoff games? And we did it in five consecutive years."
> Denis Potvin

But it all came crashing down with the Islanders on the verge of tying the Montreal Canadiens' record five straight Stanley Cups from 1956 to 1960. New York met the Edmonton Oilers in the 1984 Cup final and there was no love lost between the teams. They had met in the 1983 final, with the veteran Islanders sweeping the green Oilers. But by the '84 final, the tide had turned: Edmonton was a dynasty in the making.

The Oilers had scored a record 424 goals that season, 122 more than New York. With 196 points, Wayne Gretzky won the NHL scoring title by 72 points. Mark Messier, Jari Kurri and Glenn Anderson, all scored 45-plus goals and 100-plus points. Defenseman-by-title-alone Paul Coffey rounded out Edmonton's top five with 96 points and four other Oilers managed 19 or more goals.

They had an air of cockiness about them. And although New York's greats were just five or so years senior to Edmonton's, the Islanders were seemingly of a different generation. They didn't take kindly to the Oilers ways and weren't afraid to let it be known.

But it was too much too late. After all the games, series, All-Star Games and Canada Cups, New York was just plain worn out. Edmonton won the Cup in five games, outscoring the Islanders 25-8.

"Consider this," Potvin said, "Montreal won five Cups by winning 10 playoff series...I think we played 120 playoff games in five years. How many NHLers in history have played 120 playoff games? And we did it in five consecutive years."

The five most successful years in NHL playoff history.
∎ John Grigg

GOALS IN ONE PLAYOFF SERIES [JARI KURRI, 12]

049

Hall of Famer Jari Kurri had a career year in 1984-85 with the Oilers, setting a personal high with 71 goals during the regular season and tying Reggie Leach's mark of 19 goals in one post-season. Kurri can thank the potent offense around him and a porous Chicago Black Hawks defense for his playoff achievement.

The Finn scorched the Hawks for 12 goals during the Campbell Conference final, breaking the previous record held by Montreal's Newsy Lalonde. Lalonde scored 11 in five contests against the Ottawa Senators in 1919, just the second year of the NHL.

The Oilers and Hawks combined for an NHL-record 69 goals in a series where Kurri scored two goals in an 11-2 win in Game 1, three in a 7-3 victory in Game 2, another three in a 10-5 route in Game 5 and four in the 8-2 clincher in Game 6. His three hat tricks in one series is also a record.

SEASONS IN THE PLAYOFFS
[CHRIS CHELIOS, 24]

More than 6,000 men have skated in an NHL playoff game, but only one, Chris Chelios, did it in 24 different seasons.

It all began for Chelios in 1984 when, after playing for the U.S. Olympic Team in Sarajevo, he joined the Montreal Canadiens, who had drafted him 40th overall in 1981.

"I knew I wasn't ready for the NHL (in 1981)," Chelios told THN prior to the 1984-85 season. "I thought I was ready to turn pro after one year (of college), but then I realized the Olympics were a once-in-a-lifetime chance. So I put it off again."

Chelios got his feet wet at the end of the '83-84 season, playing 12 games for the Habs before the post-season. During Montreal's run to the Wales Conference final, the 22-year-old was one of the team's strongest blueliners defensively and finished second in Canadiens playoff scoring with a goal and 10 points.

In his remarkable 26-year career, Chris Chelios claimed three Cups and three Norris Trophies.

"When I went to Montreal, they did a lot to help me with my confidence," Chelios said. "Going into the playoffs, I think I had two points. But they still played me and eventually things started clicking."

And they rarely stopped clicking. Chelios' teams made the playoffs the first 14 chances they had during his career and he won a Stanley Cup with Montreal in 1986 and three Norris Trophies before finally missing the post-season 1998 with Chicago.

"I don't know what it's like to not make the playoffs," Chelios told THN as the '98 season was coming to a close, "but I know it's not a good feeling."

> ## "I don't know what it's like to not make the playoffs, but I know it's not a good feeling."
> ### Chris Chelios

He wouldn't have to feel that bad again for quite some time. With his hometown Blackhawks bottoming out again in 1999, Chelios was traded to Detroit. The Red Wings qualified for each of the next 10 post-seasons and Chelios was there for all of them, winning two more Cups.

The run finally ended in 2010 when Chelios, who spent most of the season with the Chicago Wolves of the American League, played seven games with the Atlanta Thrashers, who, as usual, missed the post-season. The final, impressive tally: 26 seasons, 24 in the playoffs...and an NHL record to boot.

POINTS IN ONE PLAYOFF GAME

[PATRIK SUNDSTROM AND MARIO LEMIEUX, 8]

051

Wayne Gretzky and Mario Lemieux were compared to each other throughout their illustrious careers, so it didn't surprise many when Lemieux climbed past one of The Great One's records during the 1989 Stanley Cup playoffs. But the fact Patrik Sundstrom was already at the top when Mario got there raised a few eyebrows and dropped a few jaws.

On April 22, 1988 Sundstrom set the record for most points in a playoff game when he picked up eight (three goals) in a 10-4 win in Game 3 of the Devils' series with Washington. The Skelleftea, Sweden, native assisted on all four of linemate Mark Johnson's tallies and Sundstrom picked up the record-breaking point with his hat-trick goal at the 14:14 mark of the third period.

Sundstrom's record didn't stand alone for long, though, as almost a year to the day later, on April 25, 1988, Lemieux tied the mark with a huge night against the Flyers in a 10-7 Penguins win. It took 'Super Mario' less than seven minutes to score a natural hat trick in game in which he also tied the record for most goals in one playoff game when he potted an empty-netter for his fifth of the night.

Including the regular season, only 12 players have scored eight or more points in a single game. Gretzky did it twice, Lemieux three times.

052

FEWEST GOALS SCORED IN THE PLAYOFFS BY A STANLEY CUP WINNER (FOUR ROUNDS)
[MONTREAL CANADIENS, 56]

Rookie Patrick Roy's Conn Smythe-winning performance during the 1986 playoffs is even more impressive because no team has scored fewer goals over four rounds to win a championship. He needed to be clutch as the Habs only managed 2.8 goals per game in an era when the Cup winner usually averaged more than four.

Montreal's 56 goals were paced by another rookie, Claude Lemieux, who tallied 10 markers. Only three other Habs managed more than five in the 20 games and no one averaged a point a game. Roy had to be their best player every night; eight of their 15 wins (Round 1 was a best-of-five affair) came by one goal and they only managed four scores in their five losses.

The 1975-76 Canadiens scored just 44 times en route to a Cup, but their first-round bye meant only playing 13 games over three rounds instead of four.

▶ Claude Lemieux's 10 markers was just enough offense to lead the Montreal Canadiens to their 23rd Stanley Cup in 1986.

Bruin something special

PLAYERS WITH 20 OR MORE GOALS IN ONE SEASON
[BOSTON BRUINS, 11]

053

I t was two years after the breakup of The Big Bad Bruins (no more Bobby Orr or Phil Esposito) and a year before the infamous Too Many Men on the Ice call in the 1979 Stanley Cup semifinal at Montreal.

In between, the 1977-78 Boston Bruins were the team of So Many Men with 20 goals or more – an NHL-record 11.

"They all played hard, so I thought it was possible for any one of them to score 20," said Johnny Bucyk, the Hockey Hall of Famer who played his final season in '77-78 and, because of injuries, wasn't on the 20-goal list. "But I guess I never thought I'd see all 11 score 20 goals in the same year."

Those Don Cherry-coached Bruins beat the record of 10 set by Boston's 1970-71 team, which had a record four 100-point scorers.

The Bruins scored 333 goals - 115 more than they surrendered - during a 51-18-11 campaign.

Predictably, the 1977-78 squad featured a couple of future Hall of Famers in Jean Ratelle (25 goals) and Brad Park (22), a pair of ex-Rangers who came to Boston in exchange for Esposito and Carol Vadnais. Another former Ranger, Rick Middleton, scored 25 times for the Bruins in '77-78 – the fourth of 11 straight seasons he'd reach the 20-goal level.

But as was typical of a Cherry-coached team, pluggers, plumbers and grinders got plenty of opportunity to play regularly and several of them came through on the offensive end.

Topping that list was the beloved Terry O'Reilly, Boston's future captain, who didn't just score a career-high 29 goals, but also led the B's in points (90) and penalty minutes (211). Stan Jonathan, not far behind O'Reilly on the popularity scale, also had his best season, with 27 markers. Wayne Cashman, who came to prominence as the winger who dug so many pucks out of corners for Esposito, scored 24 times.

Penalty-killing expert Don Marcotte chipped in 20, as did Bob Miller, who stood out for a couple of reasons: One of the few Americans in the league at the time, the local kid (he grew up north of Boston) was a rookie – and he'd never score 20 goals again. Third-line center Greg Sheppard scored 23 times – the last of his four straight seasons of 20 goals or more.

"I never thought I'd see all 11 score 20 goals in the same year."
Johnny Bucyk

Not that Cherry had anything against skilled players. Besides the aforementioned Ratelle and Middleton, Boston got 27 goals from hard-shooting sniper Bobby Schmautz and a team-leading 41 tallies from center Peter McNab. Interestingly, on a team with 11 players hitting for 20 goals or more, McNab was the only one to pass 30 – although that probably wouldn't have been the case if injuries hadn't limited Schmautz and Sheppard to 54 games apiece.

With 10 forwards on the eclectic list of 20-goal men (Park was the only defenseman to make it), the Bruins were tough to shut down. They went 17 straight games without losing at one point (15-0-2) and scored 333 goals – 115 more than they surrendered – during a 51-18-11 campaign. Boston reached the Stanley Cup final, but lost to Montreal for the second straight year.

"We had so many guys who could score big goals for us that year," said Bucyk, whose streak of consecutive 20-goal seasons ended at 10 that season. (He hit for 20 or more in 16 seasons altogether.) "We never felt like we were out of a game. The season didn't end like we wanted, but it was a lot of fun to be on that team." ❚ Mike Loftus

FASTEST THREE GOALS BY A TEAM
[BOSTON BRUINS, 20 SECONDS]

054

The Big Bad Bruins assaulted the record books in 1970-71, but one of their milestones stands out for its time-defying, "no way" factor. The Bruins defeated the visiting Vancouver Canucks 8-3 on Feb. 25, 1971 thanks in part to when three players combined to score three goals in 20 seconds. Johnny Bucyk connected at 4:50 of the third period, followed by Ed Westfall at 5:02 and Ted Green at 5:10.

CONSECUTIVE ALL-STAR TEAMS
[RAY BOURQUE, 17]

055

There are guys who play in the All-Star Game and there are *all-stars*.

Ray Bourque was a post-season all-star nearly his entire career, 19 times named a first- or second-team all-star, including a never-will-be-approached record 17 consecutive elections.

Bourque's career began with a bang. The eighth overall pick in 1979 by Boston, he went straight to the Bruins from Verdun of the Quebec League. To say he was ready would be an understatement.

Bourque became the first non-goalie to win the Calder Trophy and be named a first-team all-star. He went on to rack up individual achievements at a rate only a handful of other NHLers can boast.

"There was a name missing from that Cup. Now everything is normal."
– Patrick Roy

The Hockey News' fourth-best blueliner of all-time according to *The Top 100 Players of All-Time by Position* in 2010, Bourque played 22 seasons and was an all-star 86 percent of them (only goalies Bill Durnan and Ken Dryden have better percentages). And only Gordie Howe, with 21 selections overall, has more than Bourque's 19. But even Howe can't match Bourque's 13 first-team spots.

And they were well deserved. Bourque won five Norris Trophies (finishing second six other times), skated in a record 19 straight All-Star Games and retired as the NHL's all-time leading scorer among defensemen.

Bourque also went out on top, winning his lone Stanley Cup in 2001 with Colorado after a move from Boston the year before.

"There was a name missing from that Cup," said Avalanche goalie and 2001 Conn Smythe winner Patrick Roy after those playoffs. "Now everything is normal."

Of course, it wouldn't have been normal had Bourque not been named a post-season all-star, which he was – and a first-teamer at that. The 40-year-old then retired and both the Bruins and the Avalanche immediately retired his number. He was inducted into the Hockey Hall of Fame in 2004, his first year of eligibility.

"I also made a strong commitment to myself never to stay too long in the game," Bourque said at his retirement press conference. "I could have played another two or three years, but I don't think I would have played at the same level."

It's true, not even Ray Bourque could be an all-star forever. Just for 17 consecutive seasons.

Say, Ray, how many Norris Trophies did you win during your career?

CONSECUTIVE SEASONS MAKING THE PLAYOFFS
[BOSTON BRUINS, 29]

For decades the Boston Bruins and the playoffs were synonymous. From Bobby Orr's sophomore season in 1967-68 until Cam Neely's retirement after the 1995-96 season, the Bruins played in an NHL record 29 consecutive Stanley Cup tournaments.

The Bruins were a middling offensive team in 1996-97, but allowed 300 goals against, 20 more than the next worst team, and it cost them. Especially in close contests.

"We let a lot of games slip away," said defenseman John Rohloff as the season was winding down. "Four goals, five goals here or there and we'd probably still be playing for something."

It all came to a crashing end in 1997.

The record-setting streak began after the darkest of periods for the Black & Gold: eight consecutive seasons out of the playoffs. From 1960 to '67, the Bruins averaged fewer than 19 wins a year and it wasn't until Orr arrived to revolutionize the game that Boston's ship began to right.

Two years after winning 17 games with Orr as a rookie, Boston won the 1970 Cup, then another in 1972. They returned to the final three of the next six seasons and once more in 1988, winning none but still giving fans long spring rides.

It all came to a crashing end in 1997, when Boston tied a franchise record for losses with 47, finishing last overall with 61 points, 30 fewer than the season prior.

Ray Bourque missed 20 games dealing with injuries and the team used six goalies, the most successful of whom, Bill Ranford, was dealt to Washington March 1 with arguably the team's most dangerous offensive players, Adam Oates and Rick Tocchet.

The season was essentially sunk with 20 games to play.

"It's hard to describe," said then 19-year-old blueliner Kyle McLaren. "There's just this empty feeling inside you. It's just an unbelievable feeling: Done in the middle of April."

POINTS BY A DEFENSEMAN IN ONE SEASON
[BOBBY ORR, 139]

057

When you talk to Bobby Orr about his career, there isn't a whole lot of new ground to cover. After all, his days as the best defenseman, if not the best player, of all-time are well documented and he hasn't played a meaningful game in more than three decades.

And he's not comfortable talking about his career, maybe because it was so abruptly aborted by aching, surgically repaired (sort of) knees.

"How do you feel when somebody tells you that you wrote a good story?" Orr responds when asked how he reacts to those who constantly tell him he was the greatest player the game has ever seen.

There is little doubt Orr was the most dynamic skater to ever patrol a blueline. He had the ability to change the complexion of a game and in doing so, changed the complexion *of* the game. Never before had the sport seen a defenseman who could have the impact in all three zones that Orr had because of his skating ability.

And during the 1970-71 campaign, Orr had the single greatest offensive season ever for a defenseman. In 78 games, he scored 37 goals and added a mind-boggling 102 assists. Wayne Gretzky managed 102 or more assists 11 times and Mario Lemieux once, but that's it, ever. Two players, both centers. Those 139 points are a total Sidney Crosby or any other forward would kill for these days, but there was Orr, a defenseman, posting them in his fifth year in the league.

Paul Coffey came within one point of Orr's 139 points exactly 15 years later, but nobody else has even come close in the quarter of a century that has passed since. Coffey did surpass Orr to set the record for goals by a defenseman with 48 that 1985-86 season, but Orr doesn't expect anyone to approach his or Coffey's numbers any time soon.

Never before had the sport seen a defenseman who could have the impact in all three zones that Orr had because of his skating ability.

"I see offense-minded guys who jump up into the play, but I don't see any young defensemen who skate like Paul Coffey," Orr said. "I remember my father would call me and say, 'Did you see Paul Coffey play last night? He can skate even better than you did.' "

Orr and Coffey have the nine highest totals for points by a defenseman in a season and tied for 10th (with Orr) on the list is Al MacInnis, whose 103 points is 10 back of the ninth-place total posted by Coffey.

For all the accolades now heaped upon Orr, his history-making 1970-71 campaign might have been the most inconspicuous great season ever.

First of all, the Bruins didn't win the Stanley Cup that year. After piling up a then-record 121 points, Boston was stunned in seven games in the first round by the Montreal Canadiens.

Bobby Orr

Also, the Bruins were an offensive juggernaut with 10 men scoring 20 or more times and Phil Esposito smashing Bobby Hull's two-year-old goals record by an astounding 18 when he finished with 76 markers.

The Hockey News published 35 issues that season and Orr was on the cover 21 times, but 19 of them were because he was in an advertisement on the cover. Not a single THN Boston Bruins story in 1970-71 was exclusively devoted to Orr. But his season didn't go entirely unnoticed. Orr won the second of three straight Hart Trophies as the NHL's most valuable player (no defenseman had won it for 27 years and Chris Pronger is the only one to win it since) and, of course, the Norris Trophy, his fourth of eight consecutive. (Three consecutive Harts by a blueliner and eight straight Norris Trophies are two more records.)

That 139-point season cemented the legend that was already Orr and helped spawn a generation of offensively gifted defensemen from Denis Potvin to Coffey to Larry Murphy to Ray Bourque. But since Orr left the game, only one defenseman has come along with the array of natural skills he possessed. That player would be Scott Niedermayer, whose numbers paled in comparison to Orr's at the NHL level because

> *"I remember my father would call me and say: 'Did you see Paul Coffey play last night? He can skate even better than you did.'"*
>
> Bobby Orr

once he reached the New Jersey Devils, he was reined in so dramatically he almost never took offensive risks.

"Now, right from the kids up, coaches don't let or want players to play like I played, which is a shame," Orr said. "Since Raymond (Bourque) and Denis (Potvin) and Larry (Robinson) are gone you don't see any defensemen coming like that now, because they're not allowed to play like that. I couldn't imagine sitting back all the time." ▮ Ken Campbell

POINTS IN ONE PLAYOFF SERIES
[RICK MIDDLETON, 19]

058

It takes a team effort to win. You've heard that before, it's one of the oldest clichés in sports. But if there was ever a case for one guy doing it himself, Rick Middleton sure has it.

The Boston Bruins sniper carried his team to an Adams Division final win over the Buffalo Sabres in seven games during the 1983 Stanley Cup playoffs and in the process set the record for most points in a single series with 19. Of the 30 goals the Bruins scored in the seven-game battle, Middleton had a hand in slightly less than two-thirds of those tallies.

The 29-year-old picked up points in every game, highlighted by a six-point night in a 6-2 Game 3 victory. Middleton finished the post-season with 33 points in 17 games as the Bruins wound up losing to the Islanders in the conference final. His 33 points still represents the highest total for a player who didn't reach the Stanley Cup final.

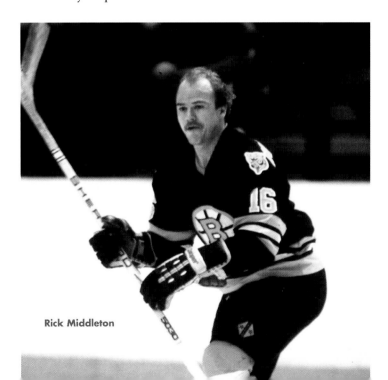

Rick Middleton

HIGHEST SAVE PERCENTAGE IN ONE SEASON
[TIM THOMAS, .938]

059

The NHL began keeping track of save percentage in 1983 and Tim Thomas became its king in 28 years later. The Boston Bruins' goaltender put the cap on a new single-season record of .938 with a 31-save performance in a 3-1 victory over the Ottawa Senators April 9, 2011 in front of a sellout crowd at the TD Garden.

One of Thomas' heroes, future Hockey Hall of Famer Dominik Hasek, previously held the record with a .937 mark, set while with the Buffalo Sabres during the 1998-99 season. That year Hasek won his third consecutive Vezina Trophy.

Thomas, the 2009 Vezina winner, was coming off an injury-plagued '09-10 season in which he lost his No. 1 job to young Tuukka Rask and had hip surgery at season's end.

"I hadn't been dragged in the mud at that level before," Thomas told THN during his record-setting campaign. "I never listen too hard to that kind of stuff, but it was hard on my family. They had to sit in the crowd when you're getting booed."

But Thomas left no doubt as to Beantown's top dog in '10-11. He had shutouts in three of his first six starts and nine in all, while finishing the campaign with a league-leading 2.00 goals-against average in 55 starts.

◄ Tim Thomas' record-setting save percentage was more than enough for the 2011 Vezina.

060

HIGHEST WINNING PERCENTAGE BY A TEAM IN ONE SEASON
[BOSTON BRUINS, .875]

Hockey was a wide-open game in the early days of the NHL. Joe Malone's 44 goals in just 20 games during the league's first season of 1917-18 is ample proof of that. But as the NHL expanded from three teams to 10 by 1926-27, defense came to dominate the game. In an effort to reverse the trend, the NHL (which had only permitted forward passing in the neutral zone) allowed teams to pass the puck ahead in the defensive zone in 1928-29.

Despite the rule change, teams combined to score just 2.9 goals per game in 1928-29. George Hainsworth of the Montreal Canadiens posted 22 shutouts and a 0.92 goals-against average during the 44-game season. The Boston Bruins won the Stanley Cup, but Boston GM Art Ross realized defensive tactics were killing the game. So Ross and New York Rangers GM Lester Patrick spearheaded several rules changes for the 1929-30 season. One new rule permitted only two players, in addition to the goalie, to remain in the defensive zone when the puck went up the ice. Another allowed players to kick the puck...as long as they didn't kick it into the net. But the most important rule change called for forward passing in all three zones.

Ross, now once again coaching the Bruins after a one-year hiatus, retained his entire Stanley Cup roster from 1928-29 with the exception of player-coach Cy Denneny and two others and had added a few newcomers as well. He originally hoped to bring the Bruins together on Oct. 14, 1929 – a full month before the start of the new season – for a week of exercises before taking to the ice for training camp on Oct. 22. As it turned out, the Bruins reported for just one day of exercises on Oct. 28 before hitting the ice the next day. Still, Ross drilled his players hard on the new rules and the results were obvious. The Bruins beat Detroit 5-2 in their season opener on Nov. 14

and rattled off four wins in a row. After dropping two of its next three games, Boston won six in a row.

At this point in the 1929-30 season, scoring was up a whopping four goals per game (to 6.91) from the previous season. The only restriction on forward passing was that the puck could not be advanced across the blueline. However, there was nothing to prevent a player from parking himself in front of the opposing goal and waiting until a teammate could pass him the puck. Boston center Cooney Weiland employed this "goal-sucking" tactic to perfection – until a rule change on Dec. 21, 1929 stated players would no longer be permitted to cross the blueline ahead of the puck. It was the birth of the modern offside rule.

In a season in which no other team won more than 23 games, the Bruins went 38-5-1.

Even with the new rule change, Boston won eight straight to run its winning streak to 14 games. Later in the season, the B's went undefeated in 17 straight with 16 wins and a tie. Weiland finished the 44-game season with 43 goals. His 30 assists gave him 73 points, which shattered the previous NHL record of 51 set by Howie Morenz two years earlier. Weiland's right winger, Dit Clapper, scored 41 times, while left winger Dutch Gainor had 18 goals and a team-leading 31 assists. In a season in which no other team won more than 23 games, the Bruins went 38-5-1 for 77 points and a winning percentage of .875 that remains the best in NHL history.

To put Boston's .875 winning percentage in perspective, consider the 132 points posted by the 60-8-12 Montreal Canadiens of 1976-77 equals only .825, while Detroit's 62 wins (62-13-7, 131 points) in 1995-96 produced only a .799 winning percentage.

But good as they were during the regular season, the 1929-30 Bruins ultimately came up short. Though Boston had not lost two in a row all season, the team was swept by the Canadiens in the best-of-three Stanley Cup final. ∎ Eric Zweig

Soft Pads, Soft Hands

SHUTOUTS BY A ROOKIE
[TONY ESPOSITO, 15]

061

Hall of Fame goaltender Tony Esposito won his first and only Stanley Cup as the third-string goalie with the Montreal Canadiens dynasty of the late 1960s.

It was a great way to start a career, Esposito acknowledges, but he played just 13 games that 1968-69 season and none in the playoffs. The Habs were led by 39-year-old Gump Worsley in net and 23-year-old sophomore sensation Rogie Vachon was his understudy. It was Montreal's fourth Cup in five seasons.

A month after the Habs swept St. Louis in the spring of 1969, the NHL held an intra-league draft as a way of re-distributing the talent. Chicago made Esposito the second pick and even though he was going to a last-place team, there were no tears.

"Absolutely not," said the man who was about to embark upon a record-setting season. "I knew the Black Hawks had the makings of a good team. I played against them with Montreal and we won 4-2, but we were outplayed. I said at the time, geez if they ever get a goaltender who could be consistent, they have a good group of forwards. They had a lot of talent."

"The shutout was a bonus, I just wanted a win."
Tony Esposito

The Hawks had high hopes for Esposito. Tony's brother Phil played for Chicago the first three full years of his career before getting traded in 1967 and blossoming with Boston. The Hawks didn't want another Esposito to get away.

"I knew Chicago well because Phil had played there when I was in college at Michigan Tech," Esposito said. "I'd drive down from Michigan and catch games."

Tony Esposito came by his 'Tony O' nickname honestly, averaging a shutout every 12 outings during his 886-game career.

But it was an inauspicious beginning in Chicago for Esposito. He was bombed 7-2 in St. Louis as the Hawks were outshot 43-31 in the 1969-70 opener. The Blues scored four third-period goals in a five-minute span. In his second start, Esposito allowed three third-period goals in a 4-1 home-ice loss to Detroit, a game the Hawks outplayed the Wings.

Chicago had earned one point its first six games that season before a trip to Montreal to take on the defending champions turned his season, career and life around.

"I remember being extremely nervous because I had two starts and no wins to show," Esposito recalled. "You know you have to come up with a good game in Montreal. That building was so hard to play in."

The Habs outshot Chicago 30-20 that Oct. 25, 1969 game, but Esposito stonewalled his ex-teammates and the Hawks won 5-0. It was the first of a modern day record-setting 15 shutouts that rookie season for Esposito.

"Frank Mahovlich told me later that's the best save he'd ever seen."
Tony Esposito

"The shutout was a bonus, I just wanted a win," Esposito said. "It was more important to have the team and coach (Billy Reay) gain confidence in me with a win."

Esposito went on to play 20 consecutive games after that win. The Hawks won 11 of them and tied three others. Three more shutouts during that stretch earned the rookie stopper the nickname 'Tony O' in parts of Chicago. Three more shutouts in a four-game span in December gave him seven in 27 starts and the rest of the league was calling him 'Tony O.'

The Hawks gradually climbed from last place to second heading into the home stretch. Esposito recorded three more shutouts in a four-game week – Nos. 13, 14 and 15 on the season – and Chicago slipped past Boston at the finish line.

Hockey fans everywhere were calling him 'Tony O.'

"We beat Detroit 1-0 in an important game," said Esposito, runner-up for the Hart Trophy that season. "I remember Frank Mahovlich blasted one at me from about 10 feet. He told me later that's the best save he'd ever seen. Funny thing is the puck hit me in the back of the leg because my pad had turned as I was coming across. My leg was black and blue for weeks."

No goalie since – rookie or not – has matched his 15 shutouts in one season.

"Someone is going to come along with the right team and the right qualifications and break it," Esposito predicts. "Records are made to be broken. It wouldn't really bother me at all. If anyone can do that, they deserve it. I'd be the first to congratulate them." ▌Brian Costello

062

ASSISTS BY A GOALIE IN ONE GAME
[JEFF REESE, 3]

When a team scores 13 goals in a game it's not that rare for a skater to pick up three assists. But for a goaltender? Well, that's an NHL high-water point.

Jeff Reese, a well-travelled journeyman who played 174 contests for five NHL teams, picked up three helpers during the Calgary Flames' 13-1 pounding of the San Jose Sharks on Feb. 10, 1993, one of just 26 games he played that season.

"Nobody really knew it was a record until the next day," recalled Reese, now the goalie coach for the Philadelphia Flyers. "I figured that maybe Grant Fuhr or Ron Hextall or Billy Smith had done it, but they hadn't. It's a nice record, but I think somebody will tie it some day."

LIGHTEST PLAYER
[PAUL GAUTHIER, 125 LBS.]

t helps for a player to be light on his feet, but Paul Gauthier takes that to a new level. Although the Montreal Canadiens goaltender only played 70 minutes in the NHL in 1938, it was enough for Gauthier, listed at just 125 pounds, to set the standard for small waistlines.

Signed as a free agent by Montreal in October 1937, he was loaned to the New Haven Eagles of the American League for cash. He was called up for his only NHL game on January 13, 1938 as an emergency replacement for starter Wilf Cude. Gauthier played well against the Chicago Black Hawks and after 10 minutes of overtime, the game ended in a 2-2 tie.

The slender stopper was a career minor-leaguer who would spend the next decade playing for a dozen teams in five leagues, missing the 1945-46 season due to military service.

GOALS BY A GOALIE
[RON HEXTALL AND MARTIN BRODEUR, 2]

onsidered two of the best puckhandling goalies to ever play, it is no surprise Ron Hextall of the Philadelphia Flyers and Martin Brodeur of the New Jersey Devils share the record for most career goals.

Hextall was the first goalie to both deliberately shoot the puck into the opposing net and score in the playoffs. His first was against the Boston Bruins in a 5-2 victory on Dec. 8 1987. His second goal came the next season against the Washington Capitals during an 8-5 Game 5 victory in the opening round on April 11, 1989.

Martin Brodeur would duplicate Hextall's feat a decade later. He scored his first career goal in the playoffs during New Jersey's first game of the opening round against the Montreal Canadiens on April 17, 1997. His second goal would come against the rivaled Flyers on Feb. 15, 2000 when Philadelphia scored an own-goal. That marker is also the only game-winning goal by a netminder.

POINTS BY A GOALTENDER IN ONE SEASON
[GRANT FUHR, 14]

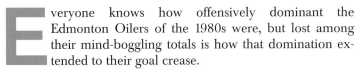

Everyone knows how offensively dominant the Edmonton Oilers of the 1980s were, but lost among their mind-boggling totals is how that domination extended to their goal crease.

Oilers goaltender Grant Fuhr recorded 14 assists during the 1983-84 season, a 0.31 points-per-game average. But while he had the No. 1 season, he's not tops all-time. With 46 career points, Fuhr is second after Tom Barrasso with 48.

The '83-84 season was a magical one for the Oilers. They pumped in a remarkable (and still record) 446 goals, led by Wayne Gretzky's 87 and 37 or more from future Hall of Famers Jari Kurri, Paul Coffey, Glenn Anderson and Mark Messier.

In the playoffs, the 21-year-old Fuhr kept up his "torrid" offensive pace with three assists in the 18 games Edmonton played on their way to their first of four straight Stanley Cups.

GAMES PLAYED BY A GOALIE IN ONE SEASON
[GRANT FUHR, 79]

There was nothing in that summer of 1995, or even during training camp, that gave Grant Fuhr any inkling that he would be the most-active goaltender in a single season in NHL history.

Quite the opposite, in fact.

Fuhr, who had won five Stanley Cup championships with the Edmonton Oilers, was coming off a season in which he had played only 17 games in Buffalo and Los Angeles. He joined the St. Louis Blues as a free agent at the urging of coach Mike Keenan and looked at it as a good opportunity with the departure of Curtis Joseph.

Fuhr's first task was not convincing anyone, least of all himself, that he could still play at an elite level. No. 1 on the to-do list was more of an off-ice factor: getting along with Keenan.

"I've always had the mentality that if players can play every night, goalies should be able to play every night, too."
Grant Fuhr

"Mike and I obviously didn't see eye-to-eye in training camp, so I didn't actually think I'd play every day," Fuhr said.

Talent, however, prevailed, and Fuhr turned in a yeoman's season, setting a record for games played (79) – breaking the mark of 70 set by Ed Johnston of the Boston Bruins 32 years earlier – and consecutive starts (76).

"I enjoyed it," said Fuhr, who was inducted into the Hall of Fame in 2003 after a 19-year career that spanned 868 games,

Grant Fuhr was a busy, busy man his first two seasons in St. Louis. The year after the record-setting 79, he played 73 games.

plus another 150 in the playoffs. "I've always had the mentality that if players can play every night, goalies should be able to play every night, too. And it's fun to play every game."

Sean Burke, who had a stellar 17-year career, replaced Fuhr in 2009 as the goaltending coach for the Phoenix Coyotes. To set those sorts of records, he said, takes a person who is strong both mentally and physically.

"It's very impressive," Burke said. "I think a lot of it, though, is…how much practice he was doing at the time, how many days off he got. The feat itself of playing that many games at that level is very, very impressive. To do that, you have to manage it very well.

"The great thing about 'Fuhrsie' is his whole demeanor; the way he looked at the game was just to go out and battle and have fun. So that kind of mentality probably helped a lot, too."

All things considered, Burke said, Fuhr probably has not gotten as much recognition for the feat that he has deserved.

"The feat itself of playing that many games at that level is very, very impressive."
Sean Burke

The 5-foot-10 Fuhr, who played at 200 pounds, did not have the wingspan of the 6-foot-4 Burke or three of the current goalies most likely to take a shot at the 79-games-played mark: Martin Brodeur (whose career high is 78), Roberto Luongo (76) or Carey Price (72). But his stature didn't stop Fuhr from winning a Vezina Trophy. He more than made up for his smaller size with great anticipation and quick reaction time.

During the 1995-96 season, Fuhr amassed 4,365 minutes of ice time with a 2.87 goals-against average and a save percentage of .903, facing 2,157 shots. In that record-breaking campaign, which also included three shutouts, Fuhr never felt he was tiring.

"The one thing when you're playing every day is it takes the mind out of it," he said. "You know you're going to play. You just prepare to play every day."

Like all great goaltenders, Fuhr had a short memory.

Case in point: Fuhr was the losing goaltender in a 1999 playoff game against the Phoenix Coyotes, giving up the game-winner to Shane Doan. Later, when Fuhr became the team's goalie coach, Doan constantly reminded him of that goal. Fuhr's response never wavered: "I don't remember that."
▮ Jim Gintonio

SHUTOUTS IN ONE SEASON
[GEORGE HAINSWORTH, 22]

067

I f you think the NHL suffered from the Dead Puck Era in the years leading up to the 2005 lockout, you should have seen what it was like during The Boring 1920s.

"I don't know how they ever got fans out in 1926, '27 and '28," hockey historian Ernie Fitzsimmons once said. "Every goal was a major occurrence."

That was certainly the case when it was scored against the Montreal Canadiens in 1928-29, when George Hainsworth recorded a mind-boggling 22 shutouts in 44 games. That was the last season the NHL prohibited passing in the attacking zone, meaning any player who scored had to dangle through on his own or pounce on a turnover. As a result, the NHL averaged just 2.92 goals per game that season and the Chicago Black Hawks found the back of the net just 33 times.

Hainsworth stepped into the Canadiens crease after Georges Vezina died of tuberculosis. He won the first three trophies bearing Vezina's name, including the one in 1929. But the most peculiar thing about that season was the 5-foot-6, 150-pound Hainsworth was upstaged by two goalies with size-related nicknames, even though just one of them was a small stopper.

Despite the fact he posted the shutout record and what would ultimately be the lowest goals-against average (0.92) in league history, Hainsworth lost the Hart Trophy as the league's most valuable player to Roy 'Shrimp' Worters of the New York Americans. Worters, whose 5-foot-3, 135-pound frame matched his nickname, notched 13 shutouts and had a 1.15 goals-against average.

In the playoffs, Hainsworth was bettered by Cecil 'Tiny' Thompson, who turned the tables on the Canadiens and shut them out twice in three games en route to leading the Boston Bruins to the Stanley Cup. All told, Thompson, 5-foot-10 and 160 pounds, had three shutouts in five playoff games that season.

George Hainsworth

HIGHEST WINNING PERCENTAGE
[KEN DRYDEN, .758]

Ken Dryden was reminiscing once about his days with the Montreal Canadiens and, the way he figured it, much of the success of the dynastic teams of the 1970s had a lot to do with the fact they had an inferiority complex.

Whenever they looked up in their dressing room, they would see greatness staring down upon them in the form of the Canadiens' Hall of Fame players. Dryden remarked that, as hard as he tried, Guy Lafleur could never be Rocket Richard or Jean Beliveau and Larry Robinson could never be Doug Harvey.

Dryden despised losing, which was a good thing since he lost just 57 games over the course of his career.

"And I could never be Jacques Plante," Dryden said. "You're just not good enough. You'll never be good enough to be them."

Posting a .758 career winning percentage might not have been good enough in Dryden's eyes, but it was good enough to be the best in NHL history. To be sure, Dryden benefited from being on the greatest collection of talent in NHL history and that he left at precisely the right time, after the Canadiens had won their fourth straight Stanley Cup in 1979.

But it's also as certain those teams were so great in large part because they had the unflappable and ultra-competitive Dryden in net. Dryden despised losing, which was a good thing since he lost just 57 games over the course of his career. In seven-plus seasons with the Canadiens, Dryden lost an average of just 8.14 games per season, once in every seven starts.

By anyone's measure, even against the legendary Jacques Plante, that's certainly good enough.

The Habs' history drove Ken Dryden and his
teammates to be the very best in the game.

Tough Stuff

PENALTY MINUTES BY A TEAM IN ONE SEASON
[BUFFALO SABRES, 2,713]

R ob Ray is the proud owner of the penalty box door from Buffalo's Memorial Auditorium. The Sabres gave him the gate when they vacated the building in 1995 and it was a fitting gift. He entered and exited through that door with more flair than any other player, never more so than in 1991-92.

Of course, if the Sabres had limited their gift giving to that season, Ray would have had a fight on his hands. That edition of the club fought for everything.

The Sabres set the NHL record for most penalty minutes in a season, racking up 2,713. Three players topped 300 minutes, led by Ray with 354. Brad May, a 19-year-old rookie, was next with 309. Gord Donnelly, an early-season trade acquisition from Winnipeg, had 305.

"LaFontaine was a dirty son of a bitch."
Rob Ray

"At the time it was a style that kind of fit our team," Ray said. "You look at it and there were a lot of penalty minutes, but there was a time and a place for it."

The Sabres averaged 34 minutes in the box per game, with help from 91 fighting majors and an astounding 60 misconducts. Only one other team had more than 38 (Minnesota, 42).

Even Hall of Famer Pat LaFontaine had 98 penalty minutes, the only time in his career he topped 70.

"He was a dirty son of a bitch," Ray said of LaFontaine. "He protected himself extremely well. He did what he had to do to survive out there, too. Everybody talks about how great a

Rob Ray was never afraid to shed the gloves...or his shirt... for a good tussle.

player, how great a guy he is and, yeah, he was, but he was a different person on the ice."

The directive to be aggressive came from the top, despite the fact two coaches led the Sabres that season: Rick Dudley was behind the bench for the opening 28 games and John Muckler took over from there. John Tortorella was an assistant.

"It was kind of the coach's personality," Ray said. " 'Duds' liked it aggressive. 'Mucks' loved it."

The Sabres obviously had their share of tough guys, with defensemen Brad Miller (192) and Jay Wells (157) also on the team. But LaFontaine was hardly the only skilled player. The Sabres could skate with anyone, boasting Alexander Mogilny and Dale Hawerchuk, while Dave Andreychuk and Donald Audette were around to fill the net, too.

Ray said early in the season the skill players thought the testosterone-fueled youngsters were nuts, but soon saw a benefit to the madness as opponents were quick to retaliate. The Sabres managed to rank second with 466 power plays and their NHL-best 22.5 percent success rate helped them finish eighth in league scoring.

"Some of the guys on the team were like: 'What the hell are you doing?'"
Rob Ray

"It took a little while before everybody would buy into it," Ray said. "Some of the guys on the team were like, 'What the hell are you doing?' What it did is it opened up so much room for a guy like Patty. Us drawing penalties and us getting things going, we were getting three-on-three situations, four-on-four situations. It opened up the ice for them back then, at a time when there was a lot of clutching and grabbing.

"These guys excelled, obviously, with fewer guys on the ice. They didn't mind it a bit. They were able to go play their game because they knew nothing was ever going to happen to them because everybody knew you had that reputation." ▮ John Vogl

070

PENALTY MINUTES IN ONE GAME
[RANDY HOLT, **67**]

With nicknames like 'The Big Bad Bruins' and 'The Broad Street Bullies,' the Boston Bruins and Philadelphia Flyers are often lumped together as the two most menacing teams in hockey's brawl-happy 1970s era.

But Randy Holt believes one characteristic separated the clubs. The Bruins, Holt said, would come out and try to bury an opponent by putting the puck in the net. It was only when their ample talent failed that the B's turned to the rough stuff. The Flyers, though, came out with a punch-first, score-later game plan that justified their notorious reputation. And Holt's distain for Philly resulted in a record-setting right.

On March 11, 1979, Holt, acquired by Los Angeles from Vancouver just a couple months earlier to toughen up the Kings, strolled into the Philadelphia Spectrum with his opinions of the home team – and one Flyer in particular – firmly established.

> *"I believe that's why Paul allowed me to get up when Ken pulled my legs out from under me."*
>
> Randy Holt

"I did not like the Philadelphia Flyers, so every time I played against them there were fireworks," Holt said. "And then of course, add in a little rat like Ken Linseman."

The chaotic conditions resulted in a first period that landed Holt 67 penalty minutes, a record for one NHL game by 10 minutes. His nine penalties in a single frame also set a new standard, though Chris Nilan holds the mark for most penalties in a game with 10.

Holt, a modest-sized tough guy who played defense, set the tone early by targeting Linseman.

"I got him in the corner, if I remember correctly, and basically tried to make his face part of the ice," he said.

Sure enough, when the period ended, the mayhem started.

Linseman may have deserved every whack he ever got, but the Flyers were the last team that was going to watch a teammate get roughed up. With one minor penalty already on the books, Holt fought Frank Bathe late in the first period and earned himself two 10-minute misconducts in the process. But unlike today when players head to the dressing room if the time they have to serve exceeds the amount remaining in the period, Holt went to the penalty box for the remaining 5:02 of the first.

He started to get comfortable by loosening his skate laces, but a couple Flyers – including Bobby Clarke – began to chirp that he might have a rough time crossing the ice to get to the dressing room. Then Holt's teammate, Bert Wilson, confirmed Philadelphia's intentions.

"He came in the box," Holt recalled, "and said, 'Wrangler, you better get your skates done up.' "

Sure enough, when the period ended, the mayhem started. Holt was getting ready to trade punches with a much bigger opponent, Paul Holmgren, when Linseman entered the fray again.

"So we're getting ready to go when Ken comes and pulls my legs from under with me," Holt said. "Imagine, you're 5-foot-10, 180 pounds against a 6-foot-3, 225-pounder and somebody has to pull your leg to give an advantage.

"Paul said, 'I saw that Randy, get up.' "

In all, Holt fought three times – twice with Bathe – earned two 10-minute misconducts, a triple game misconduct and the initial two-minute minor as the cherry on top.

Holt played 395 NHL games for seven clubs and racked up 1,438 penalty minutes. However, after making all-star teams twice at the minor-pro level, Holt only became a tough guy when he was trying to break in with the Chicago Black Hawks in the early 1970s and coach Billy Reay said his best chance of sticking in the big league was by playing the pugilist role.

Holt evolved and carved out a career. One of his stops was in Calgary, where he still resides with his wife at age 58. A proud father of three girls, Holt likes to stress his on-ice behavior stands in complete contrast to the mild-mannered way he goes about the rest of life.

Ironically, his final NHL stop was with the Flyers in 1983-84. While in Philly, Holmgren told Holt he always respected the fact he was a fair fighter.

"I believe," Holt said, "that's why Paul allowed me to get up when Ken pulled my legs out from under me." ∎ Ryan Dixon

TIME PLAYED BY A SKATER IN ONE GAME
[SERGEI ZUBOV, 63:58]

When the puck dropped at 6:40 p.m. Dallas time to begin the Stars' 2003 Western Conference semifinal against the Mighty Ducks of Anaheim, no one had any idea they would still be there after midnight. And Sergei Zubov certainly didn't know he'd get more than an hour's worth of ice time and a place in the NHL record book.

The game, which became the fourth longest in league history, went into overtime after Stars right winger Brenden Morrow tied the game at three with 2:47 remaining in regulation. There wouldn't be another goal for more than four periods, one that counted, anyway. Each team had what looked like a game-winner called back during the extra time: Anaheim's Steve Thomas in the third overtime because the net came loose and Dallas' Philippe Boucher in the fourth because the play was offside.

Zubov led all skaters, setting the record with 63:58 played, 1:49 more than Derian Hatcher. Zubov, who averaged 25:50 that season, was held scoreless with three shots and had a minus-2 rating. He was, however, on the ice for Petr Sykora's game-winner 48 seconds into the fifth overtime.

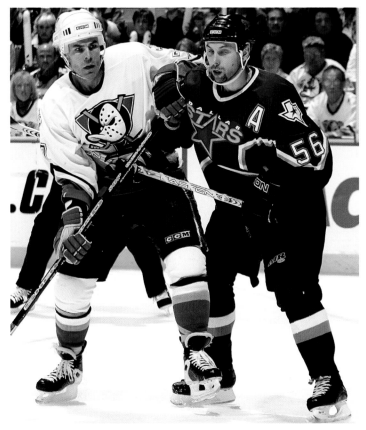

Adam Oates of the Mighty Ducks and Sergei Zubov of Dallas Stars were regular combatants in their 2003 playoff showdown.

Is Dustin Byfuglien worth his weight in gold? Pretty much. The Jets defenseman's average salary is $5.2 million; at the end of 2010, 265 pounds of gold was worth roughly $5.2 million.

HEAVIEST PLAYER
[DUSTIN BYFUGLIEN, DEREK BOOGAARD, STEVE MACINTYRE, 265 LBS.]

072

Which NHLer comes closest to breaking the scale? Dustin Byfuglien and Derek Boogaard weighed in at 265 for the 2010-11 season, according to NHL. com, while Steve MacIntyre was the same in 2009-10, according to the Society for International Hockey Research.

After using his massive frame to wreak havoc in front of the net during Chicago's Stanley Cup run in 2010, the 6-foot-5 Byfuglien was traded to Atlanta where he switched back to his natural position on defense. After a scorching start to the season, 'Big Buff' signed a contract extension almost as big as he is, worth $26 million over five years.

Boogaard was a hulking left winger for the New York Rangers and Minnesota Wild who used his size and 6-foot-7 frame to strike fear into his opponents. One of the top enforcers in the game, 'The Boogeyman' averaged more than two PIM per game over his six-season career, but you can bet that number would have been higher if others weren't so afraid of him. Unfortunately, Boogaard's story ended too soon as he passed away in May of 2011.

MacIntyre, a left winger who's bounced back and forth between the AHL and NHL, is trying to earn a reputation as a top pugilist. The 6-foot-5 Oiler has had more fights than shots in his career with 16 tilts in 76 games, many of them won in convincing fashion. He grabbed his portion of the mark last season while splitting time between the Oilers and Florida Panthers.

There were some surprising names who didn't appear at the top, notably 6-foot-3 thick-as-a-house enforcer Georges Laraque and 6-foot-9 Boston Bruins captain Zdeno Chara. But no credible source listed Laraque at more than 245 pounds or Chara at more than 260.

LOWEST POINTS-PER-GAME AVERAGE
[STU GRIMSON, 0.05]

073

n hockey circles, 'The Grim Reaper' isn't exactly a moniker that inspires confidence in one's stickhandling ability. Stick swinging? Sure. Stickhandling? Not so much.

So it comes as little surprise that Stu Grimson holds the record for lowest points-per-game average among NHLers with 500 or more games played.

Grimson played 729 contests during parts of 14 seasons for Calgary, Chicago, Anaheim, Detroit, Hartford, Carolina, Los Angeles and Nashville. He tallied 17 goals and 39 career points for a PPG average of 0.05, nowhere near his 2.9 penalty minutes per game average.

That's right, 'The Grim Reaper' found God.

But Grimson was more than just your garden-variety goon. He's always had larger causes in mind and gave generously of his time to the American Cancer Society and the Canadian and American Spinal Research Organization.

Even after being drafted twice, first by Detroit in 1983 and then by Calgary in '85, Grimson never considered hockey a viable career. Instead, he enrolled at the University of Calgary for two seasons before turning pro in 1987, the same year he found God.

That's right, Grimson found God. As an NHLer he was active in ministering and running hockey schools for Christian athletes during the off-season. And he remains faithful to this day.

After sustaining a concussion thanks to a 2001 bout with Georges Laraque, Grimson retired in 2003. He then returned to school earning a degree in economics from Belmont University in Nashville before studying law at the Cecil C. Humphreys School of Law at the University of Memphis.

In 2006 he joined the NHL Players' Association labor department. There he worked in several areas including grievances, league/player discipline and arbitrations before moving to a law firm in Nashville.

Yes, The Grim Reaper became a legal eagle; he went from defender of teammates to defender of justice, from soliciting fights to soliciting justice.

Stu Grimson

But, just because you're more likely to find him heading towards a jury box than a penalty box theses days, please don't tell him we dredged up his less-than-desirable NHL record.

074

PENALTY MINUTES BY TWO TEAMS IN ONE GAME
[PHILADELPHIA FLYERS VS. OTTAWA SENATORS, 419]

Two Flyers credos were born during their Broad Street Bullies days: 'Don't forget' and 'Don't forgive.'

Some 30 years after their brawling heyday, the Flyers still live by those standards.

Anyone who needed to be reminded received a refresher course the night of March 5, 2004 at the Wachovia Center, when the Orange and Black engaged in an extended donnybrook with the Ottawa Senators – one that ended with more total penalty minutes (419) than even those bench-clearing melees of the 1970s.

Most hockey observers agree the whole emotion-charged mess started a week before in Ottawa when the Senators' Martin Havlat used his stick to poke Philadelphia's Mark Recchi in the face after Recchi hooked Havlat.

It was an act of retaliation in the heat of the moment, but Flyers GM Bob Clarke believed it was more than that – reckless behavior with disregard for safety.

"What bothered me the most was the reflection I thought it had on hockey," said Clarke, now a senior VP with the Flyers.

"And I think I was right because it's been proven over and over again.

"Havlat was suspended for two games and said, 'It's over, I've served my time.' He had no fear in him because the league punished him. Up until the league decided to take over discipline…he would have been scared to death coming into Philadelphia, under normal circumstances."

Both Recchi and Flyers coach Ken Hitchcock were as upset as Clarke at Havlat's actions. In an interview with the CBC, Hitchcock foreshadowed: "Someday, someone's going to make him eat his lunch. This is something, in my opinion, that the players should take care of."

"Havlat would have been scared to death coming into Philadelphia, under normal circumstances."
Bobby Clarke

Added Recchi: "It doesn't surprise me coming from this guy. He's that type of player. He's done it before. It might not come from our team, but he better protect himself."

Turns out it was the Flyers who exacted revenge when things got out of control in the third period of the rematch with Philly leading 5-2. It started almost innocently with two usual suspects, Flyer Donald Brashear and the Senator Rob Ray, dropping the gloves.

But a funny thing happened on the way to the penalty box. Everyone else on the ice, 10 players in all including goaltenders Robert Esche of Philadelphia and Patrick Lalime of Ottawa, squared off.

Order was finally restored, but only briefly. A fight between Philadelphia's Michal Handzus and Ottawa's Mike Fisher touched off a second round, with the Flyers' Patrick Sharp and the Senators' Jason Spezza the key combatants.

By the time the brouhaha was over a whopping 20 players had been sent to the showers, leaving just five skaters on the benches, combined. Off-ice officials needed 90 minutes to sort out all the penalties. The damage: Flyers, 213 minutes; Senators, 206.

After the game, Clarke was incensed with Ottawa coach Jacques Martin for breaking the hockey code, which says you don't send out enforcers to fight skill players. Clarke believed Martin ordered tough guy Chris Neil to go after Radovan Somik and Mattias Timander.

"I don't think a guy like that should send players out to beat the crap out of players who can't fight," Clarke said at the time.

"What Neil did is not something to be proud of. I'm ticked off that a player like Neil would go after a player like Somik. If Martin says it's not his responsibility, then he doesn't have control of his bench."

Clarke was a key character on those '70s Bullies teams and while he didn't always play by the book, he says he knows right from wrong.

"What the league is doing with these suspensions, it's not working," he said. "The players who get suspended say they aren't going to change. Players have no fear on the ice because their opponents can't get even."

For one night, though, an effort to get even resulted in an NHL record. ▌Wayne Fish

Fare game

On that magical night in February, Darryl Sittler scored a full 10 percent of the 100 points he chalked up in the 1975-76 season.

POINTS IN ONE GAME
[DARRYL SITTLER, 10]

075

Professional athletes are known for keeping strict routines on game day and Darryl Sittler was no exception.

However, on Feb. 7, 1976, the Toronto Maple Leafs captain found himself scrambling to get home and his normal routine went out the window.

"We had our morning skate and I had some errands to run afterward," Sittler said. "I wanted to get home and have my pre-game sleep and I was running a little bit late. My wife Wendy wasn't home so rather than make a meal for myself, I stopped at Swiss Chalet and grabbed one of their half-chicken meals with fries. I had it on the seat of my car and I was eating it while I was driving home. Normally I'd go home and have some pasta with cheese and light tomato sauce or perhaps a breast of chicken."

> *"I didn't realize the magnitude of what I had done for a long time."*
> Darryl Sittler

Clearly the improvised pre-game meal didn't hurt. Sittler joined his teammates at Maple Leaf Gardens for a game against the Boston Bruins, where he proceeded to have one of the most magical nights in NHL history by scoring six goals and adding four assists for 10 points in an 11-4 victory.

The Bruins went with seldom-used third-string goaltender Dave Reece that evening, but Sittler and the Leafs had no idea anything unusual was unfolding through the first 20 minutes. Toronto took a 2-1 lead with Sittler drawing assists on goals by Lanny McDonald and Ian Turnbull.

"After the second period, our statistician said, "Darryl, if you get one more you'll tie Rocket's record.' I went out in the third period and scored three goals."

Darryl Sittler

Early in the second period, however, Sittler's big night started to really take shape. He scored at 2:56 to make it 3-1 and then set up defenseman Borje Salming 37 seconds later. Suddenly it was 4-1 and Sittler was in on all four goals. The Bruins scored at 5:19, but Sittler responded with two more goals at 8:10 and 10:27. At the end of the period Sitter was sitting with three goals and seven points – an incredibly good night's work by any standard.

He wasn't done yet, though.

"I'd had six points in a game before, but I'd never had a seven-point game," Sittler recalled. "Our statistician, Stan Obodiac, came down to the dressing room after the second period and said, 'Darryl, I don't know if you know this, but Rocket Richard has the NHL record of eight points in a game in 1944 and if you get one more you'll tie Rocket's record.' I went out in the third period and scored three goals."

Indeed he did. Sittler scored the only three markers in the third period as fans across Canada watched in amazement.

"Any time the Leafs were playing against an Original Six team on a Saturday night on *Hockey Night In Canada*, there was a real buzz in the arena," Sittler said. "Prior to that game (owner) Harold Ballard put horns behind both nets and they would wail after every goal. They got a lot of use out of the horns that night. It was kind of annoying, actually."

Sittler is proud of his record and wonders if it'll ever be broken.

"I didn't realize the magnitude of what I had done for a long time," Sittler said. "Here we are 35 years later and the record still stands. Think about all the great players who have gone through their careers, guys like Wayne Gretzky and Mario Lemieux. They both had a few eight-point games, which really isn't that far off the record.

"With the goalie's equipment being bigger and the checking being tighter, it will be a hard record to beat, but who knows? That's what makes sports so fascinating. I imagine when Rocket got eight points nobody imagined somebody would come along and get 10."

Sittler's special evening was immortalized in a children's book called *My Leafs Sweater* by Mike Leonetti.

"That book has sold thousands of copies and even though I have been retired since 1985, I still have kids come up to me today telling me it's their favorite bedtime story and I'm their favorite player because they read about my 10-point game all the time," Sittler said. "That's kind of cool." ▌Mike Brophy

CONSECUTIVE GOALS BY A TEAM IN ONE GAME
[DETROIT RED WINGS, 15]

When a goalie makes 43 saves in a game, he's typically lauded for a great night's work. That wasn't the case for Ken McAuley on Jan. 23, 1944 – not after he'd surrendered 15 goals to the Detroit Red Wings.

McAuley, who posted a 6.24 goals-against average while playing all 50 games for the Rangers that season, was the losing netminder in the worst shutout drubbing in league history, a 15-0 obliteration.

Of course, the Wings didn't earn any marks for sportsmanship. Even after they were up 10-0 with six minutes to play they were relentless, scoring five more times, including a hat trick by Syd Howe. Every Red Wings' player – with the exception of goalie Connie Dion and defenseman Cully Simon – picked up at least one point. At the other end, Dion made an "astounding" nine saves for his only career shutout.

New York didn't win another game that season and finished with only six victories, cementing its spot in last place.

077

GOALS IN ONE ROAD GAME
[RED BERENSON, 6]

n its heyday, the Spectrum was the most intimidating arena in the NHL, a raucous house of pain that sometimes caused visiting players to miss games due to the "Philly Flu."

But it wasn't always that way. Certainly it felt warmly welcoming for St. Louis Blues sniper Red Berenson the night of Nov. 7, 1968. In front of just 9,164 spectators in a game against the second-year Flyers, Berenson accomplished an offensive feat unmatched in league history, doing something not even Wayne Gretzky or Mario Lemieux managed: he collected six goals – and did it in a road game.

The night started slowly for Berenson, who had just three goals in 12 games that season. Flyers netminder Doug Favell, coming off a five-game absence due to injury, stopped Berenson's first shot and didn't surrender his first goal until 16:42 of the first period.

For Berenson, that ice-breaker was a huge relief.

"After the goal I said to myself, 'Thank God I can still score,'" he said.

The game propelled Berenson to a career year.

It took about another 15 minutes of playing time for Berenson to connect on goal No. 2, midway through the second. Then Favell saw Red. Time and time again. Berenson scored four middle-period markers and added one in the third, setting his record on just 10 shots. By the time he'd gotten to four goals, the sparse road crowd was cheering him on.

Typical of hockey players, Berenson – who netted the first five goals of the game – deflected the credit to his teammates. The then 28-year-old also thought he could have done better if

Gordon 'Red' Berenson turned the goal light red six times against the Flyers on Nov. 7, 1968.

he'd had more touch. He remembers hitting one post and just missing on several other quality chances: "It easily could have been seven or eight."

At the same time, like the polite Saskatchewan kid he was, he had comforting words for Favell following the 8-0 drubbing, noting the stopper didn't play that poorly.

"Three of the goals were on breakaways and he was screened on another," Berenson said.

Favell, who in his second NHL season was sharing crease duties with a young Bernie Parent, felt snake-bitten, done in partially by the sophomore jinx.

"I'm starting to believe in that jazz," he said at the time.

The game propelled Berenson to a career year. He finished eighth in league scoring with 35 goals and 82 points in 76 games and was the only member of the Western Division – which was comprised of the six expansion teams – to crack the top 10 point-getters.

"I think my teammates were a lot more excited about the record than I was."

Red Berenson

Playing on a club with future Hall of Famers Doug Harvey, Jacques Plante and Glenn Hall, as well as Ab McDonald, Al Arbour and Barclay Plager, Berenson was surrounded by veteran savvy – and exuberance.

"I think my teammates were a lot more excited about (the record) than I was," Berenson told THN in 1989. "I'm very surprised Wayne Gretzky or Mario Lemieux hasn't equaled the record, but I won't be surprised when they do."

With 'The Great One' and 'Super Mario' long retired, and the high-flying, high-octane offensive ways of the 1980s and early 1990s a distant memory, it could be a long while before anyone matches Red's road six-pack. ▌Jason Kay

GOALS BY A DEFENSEMAN IN ONE GAME
[IAN TURNBULL, 5]

078

The controversy surrounding the trade that brought Phil Kessel to the Maple Leafs from the Bruins lingers like uranium in Toronto because of the first round picks that were surrendered. Once upon a time, however, the scenario was reversed.

Towards the end of 1972-73, Toronto sent Hall of Famer Jacques Plante to Beantown, along with a third round draft pick, for a first-round choice and future considerations. Plante played eight games for the B's. The Leafs spent the No. 15 overall selection on Ian Turnbull.

The offense-minded defenseman from Montreal went on to become the fourth-highest point-getter among blueliners in franchise history, collecting 112 goals and 414 points in 580 games. The most memorable of those contests, by far, was his record five-goal night in a 9-1 drubbing of Detroit on Feb. 2, 1977.

"It was like a good day at the racetrack. I wish that the racetrack had been going this afternoon. I probably would have cleaned up."

Ian Turnbull

Turnbull's outburst was remarkable for a variety of reasons. First, he entered the game in a slump, having scored just three times in 35 games. Secondly, he connected for the five goals on five shots. Finally, he accomplished it against two veteran stoppers: Ed Giacomin and Jim Rutherford.

Turnbull couldn't identify exactly what led to his explosion. "I didn't do anything differently," he said after the game. "It was one of those nights when everything goes in. It was like a good day at the racetrack. I wish that the racetrack had been going this afternoon. I probably would have cleaned up."

That his feat stands alone also makes it extra special. It's something Bobby Orr, Doug Harvey, Ray Bourque and Paul Coffey never achieved.

079

BEST PLUS-MINUS RATING
IN ONE GAME
[TOM BLADON, PLUS-10]

A blowout 11-1 victory by Philadelphia over the Cleveland Barons on Dec. 11, 1977 proved to be a historic night for Flyers blueliner Tom Bladon – on more than one front.

On that night Bladon set the NHL record for best plus-minus rating in one game at plus-10. And while you certainly wouldn't confuse Bladon with the great Bobby Orr, the defenseman known as 'Bomber' did become the first player to break one of Orr's 14 NHL records with his eight-point night (four goals) against the Barons. (The Oilers' Paul Coffey would later tie the mark in 1986.)

All of Bladon's eight points were even-strength – tying Maurice Richard's record – and he was on the ice for 10 of the Flyers' 11 goals. The Barons' lone goal came with Bladon on the bench.

A plethora of points
kept pushing up Tom
Bladon's plus rating
on Dec. 11, 1977.

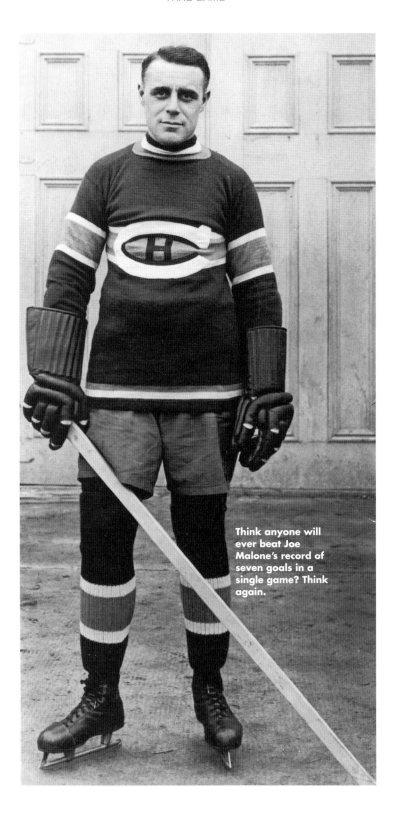

Think anyone will ever beat Joe Malone's record of seven goals in a single game? Think again.

GOALS IN ONE GAME
[JOE MALONE, 7]

080

Newsy Lalonde held the NHL record for goals in a game for exactly three weeks – and the last person he probably thought could break it that season was Joe Malone.

Malone was one of the greatest goal-scorers the game has ever seen to be sure, but he played for the pathetic Quebec Bulldogs, who won just four games that season and averaged more than seven goals against per game. But in two of those four wins, Malone scored 13 goals, including seven in a 10-6 win over the Toronto St. Patricks on Jan. 31, 1920.

Malone was one of the greatest goal-scorers, but he played for the pathetic Quebec Bulldogs.

Malone, who scored 44 goals in just 20 games two seasons before, was the lone bright light for the Bulldogs that season. He finished the year with a league-high 39 goals, while no other player for the Bulldogs scored more than 11. In fact, his six assists gave him 45 points, meaning he had a hand in almost half of his team's 91 total goals. Granted, games in the NHL were averaging 9.58 goals per contest that season and in addition to Malone's seven-goal game and Lalonde's six-goal effort, Malone also scored six in a 10-4 win over the Ottawa Senators less than two months after establishing the record.

No player has scored six goals in a game since Darryl Sittler did it 35 years ago, so it's doubtful Malone's mark will be approached anytime in the foreseeable future. In fact, seven goals is considered a decent month for a scorer in today's NHL.

081

GOALS BY A TEAM IN ONE PERIOD
[BUFFALO SABRES, 9]

Following the second period of a March 19, 1981 contest between the Buffalo Sabres and the Toronto Maple Leafs, you could hardly blame Leafs goalie Michel 'Bunny' Larocque for getting a little angry at his teammates – and himself – as the Sabres had a frame for the ages at his expense.

Larocque was mercifully pulled for the third period after Buffalo lit him up for nine goals in the middle stanza, including a hat trick by future Hall of Famer Gilbert Perreault. In total, the Sabres collected 23 individual points in the 20 minutes alone.

Larocque was replaced by backup Jiri Crha, who kept the game moderately close as the Leafs went on to lose 14-4. Andre Savard, who finished the game with three goals and six points, led Buffalo's scoring stampede. Two days later, the Sabres would rub salt in the wound once again by defeating the Leafs, this time by a 6-2 margin.

And Howe!

082

CONSECUTIVE YEARS TOP-FIVE IN SCORING
[GORDIE HOWE, 20]

O pen the NHL record book and there are still a litany of listings in which Gordie Howe tops the charts more than 30 years after he finally hung up the blades to conclude an unparalleled 26-season NHL career.

Yet there is one record on Howe's resume that stands above all the others in its combination of excellence and endurance. For 20 consecutive seasons – from the 1949-50 campaign through the 1968-69 season – Howe rated among the league's top five scorers.

Think about that. Two decades of dominance.

"You've got to say he's likely the greatest hockey player that ever played," suggested fellow Hall of Famer Bobby Hull.

Joe Louis was heavyweight boxing champion of the world when Howe launched his streak. Joe Frazier wore the belt when it came to its conclusion.

During his roll, Howe won six Art Ross Trophies as NHL scoring champion, was runner-up once, finished third five times, was fourth on two occasions and came home fifth in six seasons.

"You've got to say he's likely the greatest hockey player that ever played."

Bobby Hull

Prior to Howe, the NHL mark for the most consecutive years in the top five scorers was held by Ottawa Senators left winger Cy Denneny, who did it six seasons in a row from 1920-21 to 1925-26. The only one to make a serious run at Howe since was Wayne Gretzky, who spent 13 seasons among the top five scorers from 1979-80 through 1991-92.

Gordie Howe is one of only 18 men to score 600 goals in the NHL.

Often referred to as the Babe Ruth of hockey, it's baseball's 'Bambino' who comes closest to matching Howe's combination of durability and longevity in North America's four major sports. Ruth finished at least third in the American League in home runs for 16 straight seasons from 1918 to 1933, leading the league 12 times.

Running back Jim Brown of the Cleveland Browns topped the NFL in rushing for five straight years from 1957 to 1961 and basketball's Wilt Chamberlain was among the NBA's top five scorers every season for nine years from 1959-60 to 1967-68.

"There have been so many years and so many exciting moments, that they all blend into one," Howe said, struggling to put his incredible tenure as a scoring threat into perspective.

That task was easily filled by others.

"When I broke in with the Red Wings in 1959, I used to tell people that Gordie was amazing for his age," former NHLer John McKenzie, Howe's teammate with the WHA's New England Whalers, told *The Canadian Press*.

"There have been so many years and so many exciting moments, that they all blend into one."
Gordie Howe

Over the years, Howe was written off more than a businessman's lunch. And then he'd astonish everyone and write another memorable chapter to his one-of-a-kind story.

Hockey people were astonished when Howe led the league in scoring at the age of 29 in 1956-57, referring to him as "the aged Howe," in press reports, but by 1962-63, when he led the league in scoring again at 35, those in the game began to recognize they were dealing with a unique physical specimen.

"We've been talking for five years about him playing defense when he doesn't score goals anymore, but that day doesn't look any closer than it did five years ago," Detroit coach Sid Abel, who was Howe's center when his scoring streak began, told *The Associated Press*.

Others were projecting previously unheard-of plateaus for 'Mr. Hockey:' "He'll play five more years and wind up with at least 700 goals," New York Rangers GM Muzz Patrick predicted to *AP* at the time. "There's no doubt that Howe is the greatest player in the history of the game."

Six years later, in the final season of Howe's 20-year stretch, at the age of 41, he posted a career-high 103 points and finished third in the scoring race.

After celebrating his 83rd birthday in March, Howe laughs at the notion that he'd ever launched such a record scoring binge: "When I turned 18, I thought, 'If I could just last one year in the league, then I could brag.' " ▌ Bob Duff

OLDEST PLAYER
[GORDIE HOWE, 52]

083

While most 52-year-old grandfathers would shy away from a game in a beer league, Gordie Howe was still plying his trade in the NHL at that age. After spending six seasons in the WHA, Mr. Hockey returned to the NHL in 1979-80 with the Hartford Whalers for his 32nd and final pro season.

Howe played all 80 games, registering 41 points and skating in the NHL All-Star Game. Not bad for a man who made his NHL debut before Bobby Orr was born in 1948 and remained in the league after Orr retired in 1978-79.

Howe famously played one shift for the Detroit Vipers, of the now defunct International League, in 1997, at the age of 69. He remains the only hockey player to appear in a professional game for six consecutive decades (1940s to 1990s).

084

GAMES PLAYED
[GORDIE HOWE, 1,767]

For a guy who failed Grade 3 twice and never even finished high school, Gordie Howe's attendance record was impeccable. That he played in 97 percent of his team's games over the course of his NHL career is nothing short of remarkable.

One of the main reasons Howe held the mark as the NHL's all-time leading scorer for such a long time was the fact that he was as durable as he was talented. Howe went five straight seasons, from 1949-50 through '53-54, without missing a single regular season game.

Ironically, though, Howe's most devastating injury occurred during that time. In the first game of the playoffs in 1950, Howe lined up Ted Kennedy of the Toronto Maple Leafs for a hit, but Kennedy avoided it at the last second and Howe went head-first into the boards. Mr. Hockey sustained a fractured skull, a concussion, a broken nose and a broken cheekbone and surgeons were forced to operate to relieve the pressure on his brain. But Howe was back for the next season and played all 70 games.

Gordie Howe was as durable as he was talented.

In fact, in the 18 seasons the NHL played 70 games from 1949-50 until expansion in 1967-68, Howe missed a total of just 20 games, meaning he played in a mind-boggling 98.4 percent of the Detroit Red Wings' contests during that span.

Remarkably, Howe does not have the overall record for NHL games played, including playoffs. That belongs to Mark Messier, who has 1,992 compared to Howe's 1,924. But there are two main reasons for this. First, Howe retired for two years, then spent six more in the World Hockey Association. And for much

While most men in their early fifties dream of retirement, Gordie Howe, at age 52, played a full season of 80 games in 1979-80 for the Hartford Whalers.

In the 18 seasons the NHL played 70 games from 1949-50 until expansion in 1967-68, Howe missed a total of just 20 games.

of his career, Howe played in a league that had shorter schedules and featured only two playoff rounds as opposed to four.

The first Gordie Howe hat trick of 2010-11 was recorded by a member of Howe's old team. Wings center Pavel Datsyuk scored and assisted in a 4-0 season-opening win and dropped the gloves with Ducks 50-goal scorer Corey Perry.

He summed up the night as only Datsyuk can: "I'm happy to have the Gordie Howe hat trick, but it's not my best dream."
▌ Bob Duff

SEASONS WITH 20 OR MORE GOALS
[GORDIE HOWE, 22]

085

Gordie Howe had his first 20-plus goal campaign in 1949-50 at the age of 22 and his final 20-plus goal season in 1970-71 at 43. His season high of 49 was set in 1952-53.

Remarkably, during his final season with the Hartford Whalers in 1979-80, Howe nearly added a 23rd year to his total, potting 15 goals.

"GORDIE HOWE HAT TRICKS" [STAN MIKITA, 22]

086

The logic makes perfect sense. A goal, an assist and a fight in the same game cover the gauntlet of hockey necessities – skill, teamwork and toughness. Who better to name such an occurrence after than the man known as 'Mr. Hockey?'

While the reasoning why hockey people call this rare achievement a 'Gordie Howe hat trick' is sound, the origin of the moniker remains a mystery.

"We're not sure who coined the term 'Gordie Howe hat trick' or when it happened," said a passage on the Washington Capitals website during the 2010-11 season. "The whole thing seems kind of murky and mythic, actually."

The first recorded reference to the phrase came in a Dec. 17, 1989 article written by Frank Orr of the Toronto *Star* following a 4-3 victory by the Minnesota North Stars over the Toronto Maple Leafs the night before. "Basil McRae, who had what his mates called a Gordie Howe hat trick – a fight, a goal and an assist – gave the Stars a 2-0 lead," Orr wrote.

By the early 1990s, it was becoming a commonplace reference in hockey dressing rooms. Keith Tkachuk, who broke in with the Winnipeg Jets during the 1991-92 season, loved to talk about his collection.

The funny thing is, when it comes to the all-time leaders, Howe is nowhere to be found.

The funny thing is, when it comes to listing the all-time leaders, Howe is nowhere to be found among the group. Howe recorded just two eponymous hat tricks during his career, both against the Toronto Maple Leafs. His first was achieved Oct. 11, 1953 when Howe fought Fernie Flaman, assisted on a Red Kelly goal and scored one of his own. The other took place March 21, 1954. Howe scored the opening goal, assisted on a pair of Ted Lindsay markers and fought Toronto captain Ted 'Teeder' Kennedy.

Curiously, the all-time leader was recognized for his gentlemanly play as many times as Howe recorded Gordie Howe hat tricks.

Long before Stan Mikita combined skill and sportsmanship to win consecutive Lady Byngs in 1967 and '68, the Chicago Black Hawks center was a pugnacious sort who took guff from no one.

Four times during his first seven seasons, Mikita collected more than 100 penalty minutes and during that span he garnered the majority of his career-high 22 Gordie Howe hat tricks.

Mikita broke into the NHL playing on a line with Ted Lindsay, then the NHL's all-time penalty-minute leader and the man who ranks second all-time in Gordie Howe hat tricks with 19.

After Mikita and Lindsay, Brendan Shanahan (1987 to 2009) with 17, Rick Tocchet (1984 to 2002) with 15 and Brian Sutter (1976 to 1988) with 12, are next on the honor roll.

The 2011 Stanley Cup Western Conference final swung on a Gordie Howe hat trick by Vancouver Canucks defenseman Kevin Bieksa in Game 2 of their series with the San Jose Sharks. Bieksa pummeled Sharks forward Patrick Marleau in a first-period bout, scored the goal that put Vancouver ahead for good and later assisted on the eventual game-winner. The Canucks won the series in five games and were quick to point out his accomplishment to Bieksa.

Often, those who achieve the feat are not the ones you'd expect to deliver the goods.

"Yeah, I've heard about it," Bieksa said. "It's great, I guess. The main thing is we got the win, so that's why I'm happy."

The inaugural Gordie Howe hat tricks in NHL history came Dec. 26, 1917. Montreal's Newsy Lalonde and Toronto's Harry Cameron scrapped, while Cameron had four goals and an assist and Lalonde one of each in Toronto's 7-5 victory.

Often, those who achieve the feat are not the ones you'd expect to deliver the goods. Wayne Gretzky collected one during his career and Edmonton forward Taylor Hall, the top player chosen in the 2010 NHL draft, concluded his rookie campaign with one.

"I've never fought before and I'd never had a Gordie Howe hat trick," Hall said after scoring a goal and an assist and scrapping with Derek Dorsett during a 4-2 victory over the Columbus Blue Jackets.

They Call it a Streak

CONSECUTIVE GAMES PLAYED (INCLUDING PLAYOFFS)
[GARRY UNGER, 949]

O ften times when a car with a manual transmission won't start, drivers "pop" the clutch to get the engine going. Former NHLer Garry Unger once tried to use a clutch to pop his knee back into place.

A water-skiing accident followed by a basketball injury left Unger with a leg that wouldn't straighten out just before his first professional camp with the Toronto Maple Leafs in 1967.

"My friend had a Firebird with a four-speed," Unger said. "I thought if we traded cars and I use the clutch, one of these times my knee is going to pop back to normal and I'm going to be fine.

"By the time I got to Peterborough, I almost had it straight. Then I got to camp, we took our 'medicals' and the doctor says, 'What have you been doing with this leg?' I said I've been trying to straighten it. He said, 'Well you've been tearing it.' I had surgery on my knee and missed training camp. It was a funny way to start an ironman streak…to be hurt your whole rookie year."

Unger eventually suited up in Toronto and it wasn't until 11 years and four teams later that he finally missed a game. A streak of 949 contests, including playoffs, remains the longest in NHL history. And it could have been longer if not for a curious move by his coach in Atlanta, Al MacNeil.

Unger's determination to show up to work every day was triggered by the condition of his sister, Carol Ann, who was five years younger. She was stricken with polio as a toddler.

"I'm playing football and baseball and hockey and running around…and she was always in this wheelchair," Unger said. "So when I got an injury, it was really hard for me to say,

Garry Unger

'Whoa, I feel sorry for myself,' knowing that my sister could never get out of this chair."

Unger was traded from Toronto to Detroit and later to St. Louis, where he eventually was made aware of how many consecutive games he had played.

"We were playing in Long Island and we lost a game," Unger said. "A reporter came to me after the game and said 'Congratulations.' I said, 'What are you talking about? We just got killed.' He said, 'That was your 500th game in a row.' I said, 'That's what I do. I play hockey.' "

At the time, the NHL's ironman record was 630 games, held by long-time New York Ranger Andy Hebenton.

"As it got closer to 630, it got more publicity," Unger said. "But, again, I wasn't playing the games to try and break a streak."

Regardless, in 1976, Unger reached the milestone, an achievement that was recognized by his Blues teammates.

"They gave me a really nice Billy Cook saddle with an ironman plaque on the back," he said. "I still have it. It's one of my prized possessions."

In 1979, Unger was dealt to Atlanta and the streak came to an end in bizarre fashion against St. Louis.

"It was a funny way to start an ironman streak...to be hurt your whole rookie year."
Garry Unger

Unger said the Flames might have been the most talented team he played on, but that didn't translate to wins.

"We were struggling and every time we went into a city, because our record wasn't great, they would write about the ironman streak," he said. "I didn't know this at the time, but I guess it was bugging the coach (Al MacNeil)."

Unger had been playing with a separated shoulder, but when the Flames travelled to play the Blues on Dec. 22, 1979, he felt better. He suited up for the game, but MacNeil kept him on the bench through the first and second periods.

"He wasn't going to play me," Unger said. "With a couple of minutes left in the game, we were winning 7-2, the fans and players had realized that I hadn't been on the ice. Players were coming to me and saying, 'Take my shift.' "

In the closing seconds, a couple of sticks came up near the Atlanta bench and Unger, along with his teammates, jumped to stay out of harm's way.

"Al thought I was going over the bench, so he had a hold of my sweater so I couldn't go on the ice," Unger said. "I wasn't going on the ice. If he wants to bench me, he's just going to bench me in the next game. But people were yelling and screaming and that was the end of the streak."

Unger estimates that he played in more than 100 straight games after that game, which would have extended the streak past 1,000. He wound up playing in 914 consecutive regular season games, a mark that was broken by Doug Jarvis during the 1985-86 season. Including playoff games, however, Unger played in 949 straight games, whereas Jarvis' streak would have ended at 362 games because he missed four post-season contests in 1979 as a member of the Montreal Canadiens.

> *"It was really hard for me to say, "Whoa, I feel sorry for myself," knowing that my sister could never get out of this chair."*
>
> Garry Unger

Unger never spoke to MacNeil about the end of the streak. After his playing days, Unger didn't even see MacNeil again until early in 2011, when they had a chance encounter in the press box in Calgary.

"It was really dark up there," Unger said. "This guy walked by and I thought I recognized him. I tapped him on the shoulder and said, 'Hello,' and he turns around and it was Al MacNeil. The look on his face was worth me not ever saying anything. It was like shock. He just said 'Hello' and scurried off."

Unger still gets asked about the streak by fans.

"If I'm signing autographs, people want me to write on their picture, 'Ironman 914,' " he said. "That's pretty special."

Calgary defenseman Jay Bouwmeester holds the current NHL streak for consecutive regular season games with 506. Unger said he'd have no problem with any player breaking his record.

"If there's one record that I would hope every player who laces on a pair of skates gets to break it's an ironman record," Unger said, "because that would mean they're not getting hurt." ▌

Jeremy Rutherford

CONSECUTIVE GAMES WITH A GOAL IN THE PLAYOFFS
[REGGIE LEACH, 10]

088

Philadelphia Flyers right winger Reggie Leach's performance during the 1976 playoffs is the stuff of legends. Not only did he win the Conn Smythe Trophy – despite the Montreal Canadiens sweeping the Flyers in the final – he also set the new milestone for longest playoff goal-scoring streak at 10 games.

Leach, one of the earliest First Nations hockey stars, had a league-best 61 goals in the 1975-76 regular season and carried that magic to the playoffs. "The Rifle" shot down Rocket Richard's playoff record nine-game scoring streak, playing alongside Bobby Clarke and Bill Barber on the Flyers' L-C-B line.

Leach scored in every contest starting with the final four games against Toronto in the quarterfinal, through all five games against Boston in the semis and in Game 1 of the Cup final against Montreal. His most impressive outing came in Game 5 against the Bruins, when Leach tallied five times for the Flyers' in the 6-3 series-clinching win. In all, Leach scored 19 playoff goals.

Mario Lemieux was one of four Penguins to have 100 or more points in the 1992-93 season. 'The Magnificent One' led them all with 160.

CONSECUTIVE WINS BY A TEAM [PITTSBURGH PENGUINS, 17]

089

They were a steamroller stopped by a field mouse, but along the way they set a remarkable record.

The 1992-93 Pittsburgh Penguins were machine-like in their power and precision, a club everyone expected to win its third consecutive Stanley Cup. Their 119 points were most in franchise history and 10 more than the NHL's No. 2 team, earning them their first and only Presidents' Trophy as regular season champs.

Pens captain Mario Lemieux had one of the greatest individual campaigns in NHL history. He missed 24 games battling Hodgkin's disease, but returned to win the scoring title by 12 points, the Hart Trophy as MVP, the Masterton for perseverance and dedication, the Pearson as his peers' pick as best player and was named a first-team all-star at center.

The 1992-93 Pittsburgh Penguins were machine-like in their power and precision.

Other individual standouts included goalie Tom Barrasso, left winger Kevin Stevens and defenseman Larry Murphy, who each earned second-team all-star nods. And four Pens – Lemieux, Stevens, Rick Tocchet and Ron Francis – had 100 or more points. Stevens tallied 55 goals, Tocchet 48. Toss in future Hall of Famers Jaromir Jagr and Joe Mullen and legendary coach Scotty Bowman and you've got a more than formidable squad.

It all added up to a 56-win regular season, a record 17 of which came consecutively down the stretch.

That's what made Pittsburgh's second-round, seven-game Patrick Division setback to the New York Islanders – a team that squeaked into the post-season with 32 fewer points than the Pens and was missing its best player in Pierre Turgeon – so crushing.

"I just remember before that series against Pittsburgh, (coach) Al Arbour asking each one of us one at a time whether we could win or tie a shift versus Lemieux," said Glenn Healy, then the Islanders starting netminder and now a CBC analyst. "And then when we got to the 12th or 13th man he said: 'Good. There's the first period.' And then he started all over again."

The upset is considered one of the most shocking in league annals.

Healy remembers the end of Game 7 like it was yesterday. With the Isles up 3-1 with just a few minutes to play, Lemieux and New York defenseman Uwe Krupp got into a slashing contest and were both penalized.

"I can remember thinking 'Ah f---, here we go. (Lemieux) is off for two minutes, we won!' And they scored two goals in, like, 20 seconds."

Despite Pittsburgh's tying effort with their captain in the box, it was New York left winger David Volek, an eight-goal scorer during the season, who provided the final act of the drama when he beat Barrasso with a slapshot in overtime. The upset is considered one of the most shocking in league annals. Not even the win-streak record could quell the pain.

"(It was) my most disappointing season...disappointing team-wise," Murphy said. "We should have won the Cup. To this day, that was the toughest loss of my career." ▌ Jason Kay

CONSECUTIVE
CONSONANTS
IN A SURNAME

090

[DAVE MCLLWAIN, 5]

n addition to the distinction of playing with four different NHL teams in a single season, Dave McLlwain's Scottish surname has the most consecutive consonants in NHL history: five right off the hop.

The Pittsburgh Penguins draft pick played for six teams during parts of 10 seasons, including Winnipeg (three games), Buffalo (five), the Islanders (54) and Toronto (11) in 1991-92. McLlwain's best season was 1989-90. He scored 25 goals and 51 points in 80 games with the Jets. In 501 career games, he scored 100 goals and 207 points before spending 12 seasons playing in Germany and Switzerland.

Dave McLlwain

Gilles Gilbert played
277 games for the
Bruins, 155 of them
ending up as wins.

CONSECUTIVE WINS BY A GOALIE
[GILLES GILBERT, 17]

091

Y ou can be excused if you don't recall goaltender Gilles Gilbert's record-setting 17-game win streak for the Boston Bruins back in 1975-76. As it happened, Gilbert's run came during one of the most newsworthy campaigns in Bruins history.

In fact, Gilbert, who posted two seasons of 30-plus wins during an NHL career that spanned 13 years, wasn't even the biggest name in Boston's net that year.

Gerry Cheevers, the man with the famous stitch-pattern mask, was the netminder making headlines as he returned to the NHL after a three-and-a-half season sojourn in the rival WHA. With Cheevers back from the Cleveland Crusaders, the Bruins were looking straight ahead at a Stanley Cup, particularly since their team had been sufficiently bolstered earlier in the campaign by one of the bigger trades in history.

Gone were Phil Esposito and Carol Vadnais and in from the New York Rangers were Brad Park and Jean Ratelle. Even though Park was a hated man in Boston, he and Ratelle were both embraced heartily by the locals once they shed their blue shirts and got the B's winning.

And win they did. Behind bombastic coach Don Cherry, the Bruins took first place in the Adams Division, slid by the L.A. Kings in seven games in the quarterfinal before falling in five to the mighty Philadelphia Flyers in the next round.

Gilbert finished the campaign with a 33-8-10 record, while going 3-3 in the playoffs. His 17-game win streak bested the previous mark of 14 held by four different goalies, among them former Bruins Tiny Thompson and Ross Brooks.

Shooting Gallery

SEASONS OF 30 OR MORE GOALS
[MIKE GARTNER, 17]

092

Some scoring records are obvious. You see the mark you are aiming for and you pass it – ta da! – you are the new record holder.

Other kinds of accolades sneak up on you. That was case with Mike Gartner, whose desire for consistency got his name into the record book. A gifted right winger with blazing speed, Gartner played 19 years in the NHL scoring 30 or more goals in 17. There have been more prolific players in the history of the NHL, but none put together more seasons of 30 or more goals.

What makes Gartner's accomplishment even more remarkable is the fact he popped 30-plus goals in each of his first 15 seasons.

"You just want to play and score as much as you can."
Mike Gartner

"I don't think you have those aspirations when you first make it to the NHL," said Gartner, inducted into the Hall of Fame in 2001, the first year he was eligible. "You just want to play and score as much as you can. I would say it wasn't until nine, 10, 11 years that you look at it and think, 'Yeah, this is a little bit of a string here. Maybe I'd better bear down and try to keep it going.' "

After playing one year in the World Hockey Association with the Cincinnati Stingers, where he managed 27 goals and 52 points in 78 games as a teenager, Gartner joined the Washington Capitals in 1979-80. He immediately established himself as a scorer when he led his new team in goals and points with 36 and 68. Gartner's best season came in 1984-85 when he fired 50 goals and 102 points for the Caps.

"I was always a very good skater and had a good shot, but the goal scoring kind of started to come a little bit in junior," said Gartner, born in Ottawa but raised in Toronto. "I really developed into more of a goal-scorer in pro and, believe it or not, I never really considered myself a pure goal-scorer. I had to try to find different ways to score and it was something I really worked hard at."

In fact, there was one season, 1986-87, in which Gartner had just six goals in mid-December. He was doing all the things he used to do, but the puck just stopped going in.

"I was thinking to myself, 'Have I lost it?' " Gartner said. "I felt like I was playing pretty good, but the puck wasn't going into the net. I just decided to keep working hard and hope it comes around."

It came around – in spades. Starting on Jan. 17, 1987, Gartner managed 25 goals in 20 games en route to a 41-goal season.

The Canucks' Kirk McLean was far from the only goalie to have to pull a puck out from behind him as a result of Mike Gartner's goal-scoring prowess.

Gartner's wonderful streak of 30 or more goals came to a crashing halt in 1994-95 through no fault of his own. The NHL regular season was reduced to 48 games because of a labor dispute. Gartner wound up scoring 12 goals and 20 points in 38 games, but returned to the 30-plus neighborhood the following two seasons when he scored 35 and 32.

By comparison, Wayne Gretzky, the No. 1 goal-scorer of all-time, had 15 seasons of 30 or more goals. Gordie Howe, who is No. 2, had 14, although he added four more in the WHA. Mario Lemieux had 11, Marcel Dionne 14 and Phil Esposito 13. Gartner didn't have one or two dynamic years like most of the game's best goal-scorers are known for. It's his consistency that made him one of the most productive players in history – and landed his name in the NHL's record book. ∎ Mike Brophy

Alex Ovechkin's name appears three times in the list of top-10 single-season shot totals in NHL history.

SHOTS ON GOAL
BY A ROOKIE
[ALEX OVECHKIN, 425]

093

I f you've watched a Washington Capitals game over the past six seasons, you've surely noticed Alex Ovechkin isn't shy about putting a puck on net.

In fact, since he broke into the league, 'Alexander the Great' has led the league in shots each season, averaging a remarkable 420.

But his shots on goal in his rookie campaign, though only the third-highest total of his career, was record-breaking. In 2005-06, Ovechkin fired 425 shots, 57 more than second place Jaromir Jagr of the Rangers. Fifty-two of Ovie's shots that season found the twine, putting him at 8.1 shots for every goal – a 12.2 per cent shooting percentage.

Since he broke in, 'Alexander the Great' has led the league in shots each season.

Looking at the past 10 seasons, no rookie even comes close to Ovechkin's gaudy number. In fact, the closest shot total by a freshman in that era was the runner-up in '05-06, Sidney Crosby, who put 278 pucks on goal. Even Teemu Selanne, the record holder for most goals by a rookie with 76, only had 387 shots.

094

MOST SAVES IN ONE PLAYOFF
[TIM THOMAS, 798]

As if Tim Thomas didn't devastate Canucks fans enough in the 2011 Stanley Cup final, he also broke a record set by one of Vancouver's favorite sons in 1994.

That spring, goalie Kirk McLean averaged nearly 32 stops per game, a record 761 saves in all, in leading Vancouver on an improbable run to the final. About a month later, Thomas was drafted 217th overall by the Quebec Nordiques after his freshman season at the University of Vermont.

After a decade bouncing around the minors and Europe, Thomas finally stuck with the Bruins as a 31-year-old and never looked back.

"My first year in Finland, I won the championship there and I had a really good run," Thomas said. "But this is a totally different level. You're playing against the best players in the world."

Overall Thomas stopped 798 of the 849 pucks sent his way in the 2011 post-season, bettering his record-setting regular season save percentage (.938 vs. .940) and leading the Bruins to their first Stanley Cup in 39 years. To add insult to injury, Thomas' saves-per-game average of 31.92 just edged out McLean's 31.71.

Thomas saved his best play for the final, allowing just eight Vancouver goals in seven games and making a record 238 saves total.

With the Conn Smythe Trophy, the Vezina Trophy and the Stanley Cup all on his resume, it would appear Thomas has done it all. Although he doesn't see it that way.

"Winning the Stanley Cup is huge," he said, "but I think in this game you always have to continue to prove yourself."

SHOTS FACED IN ONE SEASON
[ROBERTO LUONGO, 2488]

095

Roberto Luongo must have been shell-shocked at the end of the 2005-06 season after facing an incredible 2,488 shots in 75 games.

Playing behind a porous Panthers defense, Luongo saw at least 30 shots in 36 games, at least 40 shots in 11 games and at least 50 in three games, with a high of 55 in a 3-2 victory in Washington Dec. 18. But the more shots Luongo faced, the better he was: 'Bobby Lou' had a 9-1-4 record when seeing at least 40 shots, including a perfect 3-0 mark when facing 50 or more.

With 4,305 minutes played, he stared down an average of 34.7 shots per 60 minutes of action. Despite Luongo's heroics, THN named Olli Jokinen the Panthers MVP that season and Luongo was traded to Vancouver in June.

096

SAVES IN A REGULAR SEASON WIN
[JAKE FORBES, 67]

096

They called him 'Jumping Jakie' and on Boxing Day, 1925, there's no doubt that New York Americans goaltender Jake Forbes was living up to his nickname.

He was jumping. And sprawling. And diving. And, possibly, at certain points during their game at Madison

Square Garden against the Pittsburgh Pirates, wondering why the NHL would wait until the 1980s before equipping the top of its nets with water bottles.

If anyone could have used a boost of liquid refreshment, Forbes was the guy. He blocked 67 of 68 shots in a 3-1 victory by the Amerks over the Pirates, bettered only by Lionel Conacher on a second period breakaway. In the process, Forbes set an NHL standard for saves by a goalie in a regular season victory.

"The Pirate forwards bombarded Forbes from all angles, but the goalie could not be beaten," wrote the Pittsburgh *Press* in its description of the game. "Pittsburgh was putting plenty of steam into its work, the fine keeping of Forbes preventing a score."

"I can't ever recall a guy playing like that and winning."

Glen Sonmor

The performance by Forbes was one of two NHL records set that night still on the books to this day. At the other end of the ice, Pittsburgh goalie Roy Worters was equally stubborn in his rejecting of the rubber, blocking 70 of the 73 shots aimed his way by the Americans. The 141 total shots on goal set the NHL mark for a regular season game.

The Associated Press was equally impressed by the work of Forbes: "Vernon Forbes, who guards the goal for the New York hockey professionals, is regarded as a marvel of action. He is a little fellow, but nimble enough to be in every part of the goal at once."

Forbes was a journeyman NHLer who played 210 games with the Amerks, Toronto St. Patricks, Hamilton Tigers and Philadelphia Quakers between 1920 and 1933. He led the NHL with 19 wins for Hamilton in 1924-25, one of only two winning campaigns he orchestrated as an NHL puckstopper.

Like Forbes, many of those who populate the list of the NHL's top single-game goaltending performances otherwise endured relatively non-descript careers.

Whoever coined the phrase less is more wasn't likely thinking about Mario Lessard at the time. But on the night of March 24, 1981, Lessard certainly allowed the Kings to do more with less.

To say the L.A. netminder was spectacular during a 4-3 victory over the Minnesota North Stars would be a huge understatement.

"I can't ever recall a guy playing like that and winning," North Stars coach Glen Sonmor told *The Associated Press* after the game.

Lessard's 65-save performance stands second only to Forbes' effort on the NHL's all-time list for saves in a regular season victory.

"(Kings captain) Mike Murphy said I had 65 saves," Lessard recalled. "I didn't believe that."

"They fed us sugar dipped in brandy to keep us going."
Normie Smith

Sam LoPresti's NHL career was just getting underway with the Chicago Black Hawks during the 1940-41 season when he stonewalled the Boston Bruins in a March 4, 1941 game. Although the Bruins won 3-2, the story of the game was LoPresti, who was pelted with a record 83 shots, compared to the 18 handled at other end by Boston's Frank Brimsek.

LoPresti faced 27 shots in the first period, 31 in the second and 22 in the third. Eddie Wiseman beat him for the game-winner with 2:31 left in the final frame. His 80 saves is the most by a goalie in regulation.

Normie Smith won the Stanley Cup with the Detroit Red Wings in 1936 and his Stanley Cup debut came in the NHL's longest-ever game, a 92-save 1-0 verdict over the Montreal Maroons in a game that lasted 176:30.

"They fed us sugar dipped in brandy to keep us going," recalled Smith in the book *Heroes of Hockeytown*. When all was said and done, Smith was credited with a 92-save shutout, the high-water mark in a playoff win. His performance is listed in the *Guinness Book of World Records*.

The Red Wings were also involved in the game that set the standard for saves in a regular season shutout, but this time were on the wrong end of a 1-0 count against the New York Rangers. John Ross Roach turned aside 50 shots between the posts for the Rangers with the only goal of the game coming when Detroit's Bernie Brophy accidentally deflected Taffy Abel's cross-crease pass in behind his own goalie, Clarence 'Dolly' Dolson. ▌ Bob Duff

SHOTS IN ONE SEASON
[PHIL ESPOSITO, 550]

Many of the records fell once the Edmonton Oilers got their engine running in the 1980s, but a decade before that the Boston Bruins put up numbers that boggled hockey minds – especially in 1970-71.

Fresh off their first Stanley Cup since 1941, the '70-71 Bruins became the NHL's first 50-win team (57, to be exact) by scoring more than any past team ever had and any team of that era could even consider. Boston, which had become the league's first 300-goal team in 1968-69, almost became the first 400-goal team two years later: The B's scored 399 goals in '70-71 – 108 more than the Montreal Canadiens, who were next in line.

Seventy-six of those goals (then a record) were scored by Phil Esposito, who put more shots on goal that season than any player ever has – 550. Over a 78-game campaign, 'Espo' averaged a tick more than seven shots per game.

"Phil had a lot going for him," said fellow Hall of Famer John Bucyk, a frequent power play linemate of Esposito. "He had a lot of skills and ability and he had a great team around him."

"Nobody could move him. So we knew that if we got in the corners and dug out the puck, Phil would be right there in the slot and he'd be open."
Johnny Bucyk

One thing Esposito had going for him was size. At 6-foot-1 and 205 pounds, he was among the bigger, stronger skilled forwards of the era. Although not an especially fast or graceful skater, he was a master at using his bulk and long reach to protect pucks and was a great stickhandler.

"Phil could play in the slot," Bucyk said. "Nobody could move him. So Ken Hodge, Wayne Cashman (Esposito's long-time wingers) or myself knew that if we got in the corners and dug out the puck, Phil would be right there in the slot and he'd be open."

For a guy who scored as much as he did, Esposito didn't have the most powerful shot. He got his wrist shots off quickly, though, and he had a deadly backhander. Another attribute: Esposito didn't waste shots.

"Not only was he quick with his stick," Bucyk recalled, "but Phil was very accurate, too. You didn't see him miss the net too often."

As if Esposito didn't have enough going for him, he was surrounded by one of the most dynamic offensive teams in any NHL era. The '70-71 Bruins had four 100-point scorers – a record since matched by three Edmonton teams of the early 1980s and the 1992-93 Pittsburgh Penguins – with Esposito leading the way at 152 to give him the second of his five scoring titles. Next came the in-his-prime Bobby Orr at 139 (with a staggering 102 assists), followed by Bucyk (116) and Hodge (105).

"He got all those shots when the defense was allowed to hang all over him. They'd hold him, hook him, slash him – and Phil still got his shots."

Johnny Bucyk

Naturally, Boston's power play was deadly and revolved around two aspects: Orr's shot from the point and Esposito's position in the low slot. Between tips, rebounds and shots off passes from his wingers, Esposito had plenty of scoring opportunities during manpower advantages and netted 25 of his 76 goals – nearly a third of his total – on the power play.

So can anybody break Esposito's record for shots?

Washington's Alex Ovechkin came close in 2008-09, when he landed 528. He played one more game that season (79) than Esposito, who played all 78 for the B's in '70-71, so it's conceivable Ovie could threaten Espo, given the benefit of an 82-game slate. But four extra games isn't Ovechkin's only advantage.

"The thing people forget about Phil is that he got all those shots when the defense was allowed to hang all over him," Bucyk said. "They'd hold him, hook him, slash him – and Phil still got his shots.

"Do those things to a player now and it's a penalty. It makes you wonder how many shots he'd have in today's game." ∎ Mike Loftus

▶ 76 of Phil Esposito's 550 shots on goal found
the back of the net in 1970-71.

Travels & Travails

TEAMS PLAYED FOR
[MIKE SILLINGER, 12]

098

Sometimes men have a little trouble remembering things. Anniversaries and birthdays, for example, have a history of being bumped in the male brain for things such as which weekend the Super Bowl is being played on and how many paychecks have to be sacrificed in order to obtain that new set of golf clubs.

Mike Sillinger, who suited up for an NHL-record 12 teams, could be forgiven if some of the finer details of his family life have been lost in a haze of boxes and moving vans. But if Sillinger ever is asked to recall where each of his three sons was born, he's got a visual reminder to rely on: the NHL jersey he was wearing at the time.

"One was born in Vancouver, so we have the Vancouver jersey in his room," Sillinger said. "My other boy was born in Regina, but I played in Florida at the time, so he picked the Panthers along with my Team Canada (1991 world junior) jersey because he wears 16 (one of his dad's old numbers) when he plays.

"And my other boy was born in Columbus, so he's got the Columbus one in his room."

Sillinger, who retired in the summer of 2009 at age 38, has at least one jersey from every team he played with during his 1,049 NHL games – not to mention a few prior to his big-league days – framed and displayed in his Regina, Sask., home. That's why having some in his boys' bedrooms not only adds a personal touch, but helps solve the need for extra wall space.

"It's good, because you have to find a place to put them all," said Sillinger, now the director of player development for the Edmonton Oilers. "The rest are downstairs in my basement."

When you play for as many teams as Sillinger did during his career, you're bound to don some colors and logos that aren't exactly the pinnacle of high hockey fashion. His workday wardrobe took a pretty hard hit when he was dealt from Detroit to Anaheim in April of 1995. He said the original Ducks logo,

262 players have played at least 1,000 NHL games heading into the 2011-12 season. Mike Sillinger is one of them with 1,049.

inspired by the Disney movie, was one of the jerseys that could actually incite a group of hockey-playing men to discuss the need for a makeover. And it wasn't the only one.

"I'd say Nashville, too, when I played there," Sillinger said. "They're kind of funky jerseys, especially those awful yellow ones. The third jersey was a little different."

Mike Sillinger could be forgiven if some of the finer details of his family life have been lost in a haze of boxes and moving vans.

Of course, appearance never is the dominant factor in determining how fondly a player remembers a former team. For Sillinger, two of the most meaningful crests he wore came before he suited up for a single NHL game in his well-travelled career. One is the Detroit sweater he was handed the day the Wings drafted him 11th overall in 1989. In fact, that was his first jersey to find its way into a frame.

"When I was drafted, the guy who owned the Boston Pizza here (in Regina) framed it and put it in his restaurant for a few years," Sillinger said. "And the deal was when I wanted it back in my house, I would just take it. So we kind of got the idea from that."

The other sweater of great significance is comprised of the Team Canada colors he wore during the 1991 World Junior Championship, when he was his province's only representative in a Saskatoon-based tournament won by Canada thanks to John Slaney's famous slapper against the Russians.

"I have it framed, but I have it framed with the gold medal inside, which is kind of cool," Sillinger said. "I was the only Saskatchewan boy to play on that team, so it was very special."
▌ Ryan Dixon

099

PLAYERS DRAFTED FROM
A JUNIOR TEAM
[PETERBOROUGH, 98]

I n 17 years as GM of the Ontario League's Peterborough Petes, Jeff Twohey saw a lot of players mature before his eyes and head off to the NHL. One of the more surprising success stories, however, was a player who has been nothing but marquee since joining the pros – Carolina captain Eric Staal.

"When we took Eric in the first round of the OHL draft, he was 5-foot-11 and 145 pounds," Twohey said. "That's not a player we took thinking he was going to be an NHLer; he was scrawny. A lot of people laughed at us. Even his dad came up to me after and said, 'thanks for taking him, but are you sure?' "

A big growth spurt (Staal is now 6-foot-4 and 205 pounds) and a Stanley Cup later, no one would question the move in retrospect. But finding raw recruits and churning them into NHLers is something the Petes have done better than any other junior program in hockey history. All told, 98 players drafted out of Peterborough have played at least one game in the NHL and many of them were impact players.

> *"Even his dad came up to me after and said: Thanks for taking him, but are you sure?"*
>
> Jeff Twohey

The biggest stars include Hall of Famers Steve Yzerman, Larry Murphy and Bob Gainey, not to mention other household names such as Chris Pronger, Tie Domi and Rick MacLeish.

Another player who almost slipped through the cracks was Boston Bruins enforcer Shawn Thornton. Twohey only saw the tough guy play because he was waiting for another game at the rink to start. Playing as an overager in major midget, Thornton had been passed over by every tier-two team in the Oshawa area. When an opponent challenged the bench to a fight, Thornton hopped over the boards and pounded him. Twohey recalls telling the woman in the stands next to him that it looked like the kid could fight. Her reply? "He's never been beat."

It was Thornton's mom. Twohey ended up taking him in the eighth round of the OHL draft that summer.

"Cameron Mann was such a threat shorthanded that we never worried about taking penalties."

Jeff Twohey

Of course, not everything the Petes touched turned to gold. Some hot junior prospects, surprisingly, never blossomed as pros. For Twohey, Cameron Mann was the poster boy. Mann's scoring prowess didn't translated to the NHL level, but his Petes GM remembers a big-time player.

"In 1996, when we were Memorial Cup hosts, I think he had 30 goals in the playoffs alone," Twohey said. "And I've never seen a penalty killer like him. He was such a threat shorthanded that we never worried about taking penalties."

Second on the list of NHL-producing junior programs is Oshawa, with more than 85, including Bobby Orr, Eric Lindros, Dave Andreychuk and Kirk McLean. The Generals just happened to be the Petes' biggest rivals back then and Twohey doesn't think that's a coincidence.

"There was probably no better rivalry at the time," he said. "There were a lot of games between the two teams that were well-scouted, because the scouts knew it would be intense. If you weren't tough and competitive and driven, you'd have a tough night."

As an overall philosophy, Twohey tried to construct Peterborough teams with skill surrounded by toughness, by which he means competitive and long on size. Character also mattered.

"If you were a committed person and a good kid, that's what we wanted," he said.

Developing NHLers was also a team mission.

"We were always conscious of a guy's pro potential," Twohey said. "The first goal was always to win the Memorial Cup and secondly to develop players for the NHL. I guess they work together." ∎ Ryan Kennedy

---

100

NAMES USED BY ONE FRANCHISE
[CALIFORNIA SEALS, 4]

o franchise in NHL history had as many name changes as the California Seals. One of the original NHL expansion teams in 1967, the Seals went local and replaced the state with the city of Oakland midway through their first season. Before the 1970-71 season, Charlie O. Finley, the celebrated and outspoken owner-cum-innovator of baseball's Oakland A's, became the franchise's third owner in four years and renamed it the California Golden Seals. But that was it for Cali.

After six consecutive seasons out of the playoffs and a failed bid at a new arena, new minority owner Mel Swig convinced local legend George Gund to help take the team to Cleveland. At the time, Swig claimed, "Cleveland could be one of the great hockey cities in the country."

The Cleveland Barons lasted just two seasons before folding and merging with the Minnesota North Stars for the 1978-79 campaign.

In all, the franchise had four different monikers in its 12 seasons.

PLAYERS DRAFTED FROM AN NCAA PROGRAM
[UNIVERSITY OF MICHIGAN, 36]

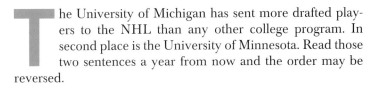

The University of Michigan has sent more drafted players to the NHL than any other college program. In second place is the University of Minnesota. Read those two sentences a year from now and the order may be reversed.

Michigan's 36 alum currently trump the Golden Gophers' 35, but with both programs still churning out NHL talent, the future leader is far from set in stone.

But what is truly outstanding about the Wolverines pipeline is the fact those 36 players come from a pool of just 49 draftees overall. Essentially, if you go to the University of Michigan and get drafted, you're probably going to play in at least one NHL game in your life.

But a healthy career is also a reasonable scenario, such as those enjoyed by Mike Cammalleri, Mike Komisarek and Aaron Ward. For coach Red Berenson – who has guided the Maize and Blue since 1984-85 – diversity is the key.

"We understand there are some forwards here that have speed, skill and are offensively gifted," he said. "But then you look at Eric Nystrom, a physical team player. Jed Ortmeyer was the same way. Johnny Madden came here as a player who could bring good offense, but terrific defense."

And neither Ortmeyer nor Madden were even drafted. They got to the NHL the hard way. Maybe that's why Berenson doesn't see the draft as a golden ticket to the big time.

"Sometimes the draft will motivate a player and other times it works against them," he said. "Especially high-round picks. I think that's why a lot of them don't pan out."

So for players who merely think they need to put on the jersey to be a star, Michigan may not be the school for you. The U of

Mike Komisarek went from Maize and Blue to Bleu, Blanc et Rouge.

M has been an institution for making the post-season. Under Berenson, the Wolverines have made it to the Frozen Four tournament 21 straight years, winning it all twice. That goes a long way in explaining how at least one Michigan player has been drafted in 17 of the past 20 drafts, despite the fact many 18-year-olds get selected before they get to college.

For Michigan alum, there's another explanation.

"I think Red Berenson has a lot to do with it."
Mike Komisarek

"I think Red Berenson has a lot to do with it," said Komisarek. "I remember my time as a stepping stone to the NHL. Obviously they know what it takes to develop guys into NHLers, but as much as Red is pushing you as a player on the ice, he cares about you and pushes you as a person off the ice. It's a great mix of athletics and academics."

The fact Michigan is a decent school also helps keep the student-athletes focused.

"You're going to school with some of the smartest people in the world," Komisarek said. "Some of these kids got 1,600 on their SATs and here you are playing hockey – it's a pretty neat experience."

And since the higher-end Wolverines often leave school early (Andrew Cogliano and Aaron Palushaj being two recent examples), Berenson's strategy of letting his recruits prove themselves early can crystallize a player's potential.

"He has a reputation of playing his freshmen in big situations in big games, in big minutes," Komisarek said. "That mentality really helps you deal with pressure moments and intense times in games." ∎ Ryan Kennedy

102

LONGEST DISTANCE TRAVELLED TO PLAY
[CRAIG ADAMS, 9,545 MILES]

Pittsburgh Penguins right winger Craig Adams went to great lengths to join the NHL – 9,545 miles to be exact, which gives Adams the record for furthest birthplace from his first NHL team.

Born in Seria, Brunei (a sovereign state located on the island of Borneo in the South China Sea) where his father worked for Shell Oil Company, Adams would've had to fly 19 hours and 49 minutes to reach Raleigh, N.C., where he played his first season with the Carolina Hurricanes.

But it wasn't a straight line, of course.

At a young age, his family relocated to Calgary, where he first picked up the sport. Adams then attended Harvard University and, after a successful freshman year in 1995-96, was taken with the second to last pick in Hartford Whalers history (223rd overall).

Adams has two Stanley Cup rings and 669 games under his belt, making the lengthy trip worthwhile.

Craig Adams' literal long journey to the NHL has been more than worth it: his name appears twice on the Stanley Cup.

103

CONSECUTIVE GAMES PLAYED
[DOUG JARVIS, 964]

Had Doug Jarvis played in today's era of heightened awareness around head injuries, there's a real good chance his games-played streak would have ended far before hitting record heights.

"There was an incident when I was with Washington, probably around the 500 or 600 mark," Jarvis said. "We were playing in Detroit one night and I got hit right at the end of the game and was knocked out in the last minute. I was taken into the locker room and I was stitched up and didn't remember a whole lot about things. We were playing the next night in St. Louis. At that time, you're checked out and everything seemed fine, so I continued on with the team and kept playing. Nowadays once you've been knocked out there's protocol."

> *"I was taken into the locker room and I was stitched up and didn't remember a whole lot about things."*
>
> Doug Jarvis

Not that he would have paid it much mind if his ironman run did come to an end. For Jarvis, who won four Stanley Cups with the Canadiens and is now an assistant coach with the Bruins, getting on the ice night after night was just part of the job.

Those nights added up, however, and by the time the streak was over he'd hit the ice for 964 straight contests, never missing a single regular season game for his entire career from 1975 to 1988. But it wasn't an injury or retirement that brought it all to a halt.

"I was into my 13th year and I played two games to start that season and I was a healthy scratch," Jarvis said. "That was the end. I never played again in the NHL. It went from my first game in the league to my last game. I felt blessed to come out all right in the end."

Doug Jarvis

104

SKATERS USED IN ONE GAME [TAMPA BAY LIGHTNING, 20]

The NHL's official rulebook stipulates no team is allowed to dress more than 18 skaters (and two goalies) for any single game. But the Tampa Bay Lightning used 20 for a contest not long ago. Why? Because of one of the more curious series of events in recent league history.

On Friday, Jan. 8, 2010, the Lightning were on the road and taking on the New Jersey Devils when, with 9:12 remaining in the second period and the Bolts holding a 3-0 lead, there was a partial power outage inside the Prudential Center that could not be fixed in time to finish the game. League officials made the decision to suspend the game and scheduled it to re-start back in New Jersey two days later on Sunday.

The NHL and the two teams agreed both rosters would remain the same for the Sunday game, but the Bolts had a regularly scheduled contest on Saturday the 9th against Philadelphia. And when Tampa defensemen Matt Smaby and Mattias Ohlund were injured in that contest, the Bolts were given permission to replace them with Andrej Meszaros and David Hale for their "rematch" with New Jersey.

The Devils had no changes to their lineup Sunday and – before a crowd estimated at no more than 3,000 – they fell to the Lightning by a 4-2 score. Neither Hale nor Meszaros had any discernible impact on the outcome, but both helped set a record that will require an even more bizarre scenario to be broken.

YEARS COVERING A TEAM
[RED FISHER, 57]

105

t's only fitting that the oldest franchise in hockey also has the longest tenured beat reporter in the sport. At the ripe young age of 84, Red Fisher has been covering the Montreal Canadiens beat for 57 years.

Initially, Fisher followed the Canadiens for the Montreal *Star* from 1954 until the paper's demise in 1979. He then moved to the sports editor's desk at the Montreal *Gazette*, where he continues to cover the Canadiens in addition to his editorial duties.

Fisher has received the National Newspaper Award for sports writing twice, while also being recognized by the Hockey Hall of Fame in 1985 as a recipient of the Elmer Ferguson Award for journalism in hockey. He was also given a lifetime achievement award from Sports Media Canada in 1999.

After covering the Canadiens through 17 of their 24 Stanley Cups, Fisher has no plan for calling it quits: "I was 27 when I took over the beat prior to the 1955-56 season. I planned to retire at 55. I'm now 84, so who knows?"

First & Foremost

POINTS BY A ROOKIE DEFENSEMAN
[LARRY MURPHY, 76]

106

Conventional wisdom amongst hockey scribes states young defensemen take longer than forwards to adapt to the pro game and develop into NHL regulars. Not so for Larry Murphy.

Drafted fourth overall by the L.A. Kings in 1980, Murphy jumped straight from junior into the NHL as a 19-year-old and posted 76 points in 1980-81, the most among rookie blueliners in NHL history.

Murphy's 60 assists in 1980-81, also a league record for freshmen defensemen, was the second highest total the rearguard tallied in his 21 NHL seasons.

Despite Murphy's record-breaking exploits, he was runner-up to 26-year-old rookie Peter Stastny in the 1980-81 Calder Trophy voting, as the Slovak center registered a 39-goal, 109-point rookie campaign for the Quebec Nordiques.

Larry Murphy had success in the NHL right off the hop.

PLAYERS FROM ONE CITY
[TORONTO, 385]

I f you had to guess which city has produced the most NHL players, you would probably get it right in one try.

It comes as no surprise that Toronto, the biggest city in the world's foremost hockey playing country, would be the birthplace of more NHLers than anywhere else. Sorry, Montreal.

The city of Toronto, not including the greater metropolitan area, has pumped out 385 young men who have laced up on hockey's biggest stage for at least one game, dating to the league's inaugural season in 1917.

Alf Skinner was the first Toronto-born player in the NHL and, fittingly, led his hometown team to the first-ever Stanley Cup championship with eight goals and 11 points in seven playoff games.

From the '20s to the late '60s, the number of Torontonians entering the NHL grew steadily until the expansion of 1967-68 caused a rush of new players to join the league.

From 1960 to 1969, 28 Torontonians started their careers as NHL hockey players. From 1970 to 1979, that number jumped to 92.

But it's been a downhill slide since, as the amount of Toronto-born players entering the league dropped to 81 in the '80s, 43 in the '90s and 35 in the 2000s.

Toronto is not alone in this regard, as other hockey havens, Montreal and Edmonton, have witnessed decreases in the past 30 years, mostly due to the growth of hockey in the United States and the European and Russian invasion of the '80s and '90s.

Outside the Great White North, Detroit lives up to its moniker as Hockeytown U.S.A., having cultivated 37 NHLers, more than any American city. Moscow, Russia, and Stockholm, Sweden, lead the way overseas with 43 and 34 players.

The city of Toronto has pumped out 385 young men who have laced up on hockey's biggest stage.

Toronto's pre-eminence in Canada's game is a given. But when you look at the amount of players born in Hogtown at a per capita level, the number is far less impressive. With a population hovering around 2.5 million, the number of NHLers per capita is only 0.02.

For the highest per capita – based on recent population measurements – among towns that have produced 10 or more pros, you have to head 600 kilometers north of Toronto to Kirkland Lake, Ont.

Kirkland Lake was once anointed "the town that made the NHL famous" by legendary broadcaster Foster Hewitt.

The gold-mining community of 8,248 (Census, 2006) is home to 22 former players, including seven-time all-star Dick Duff and six-time Cup champ Ralph Backstrom. That works out to a per capita ratio of 0.27.

Although it's far removed from its hockey heyday when it was a flourishing area, Kirkland Lake was once anointed "the town that made the NHL famous" by legendary broadcaster Foster Hewitt.

Hockey historian and award-winning author Kevin Shea pointed to the prominence of the great hockey families that first laced up on the ponds of the northern landscape, including the Hillmans (Larry and Wayne), the Redmonds (Mickey and Dick) and the Plagers (Bob, Barclay and Bill), as a tribute to the passion engrained in its inhabitants.

"A real tribute to great hockey cities," Shea said.

The last resident to make an impact in the NHL is retired goalie Daren Puppa, who lived and breathed hockey on the frozen lakes of northern Ontario as a kid.

"They had an outdoor rink at every school," Puppa said. "So we spent a lot of time out there, hanging out and playing every day."

But whether the game is played on outdoor ice or in multi-million dollar arena complexes, Toronto will always be the hockey capital of the world based on sheer numbers alone.

PLAYERS WITH THE SAME SURNAME [SMITH, 56]

108

There have been more NHLers over the years with the last name Smith than the next most common names – Brown (27) and Johnson (24) – combined. A total of 56 players with the surname Smith have suited up for at least one game in the NHL.

The all-Smith team is highlighted on the back end by goaltender Billy, who backstopped the New York Islanders dynasty and won more than 300 games; hard-hitting defensemen Steve, who had more than 2,000 career penalty minutes and is perhaps most famous for scoring on his own net in the 1986 playoffs; and Jason, who captained the Edmonton Oilers for five seasons, including their 2006 Stanley Cup run.

The forwards are led by Bobby, who won the Calder Trophy in 1979, the Stanley Cup in 1986 and is the only Smith to record 1,000 career points; Clint, a two-time Lady Byng winner who won the Stanley Cup with the Rangers in 1939-40 and led the league in assists in 1943-44; and Sid, a two-time 30-goal scorer who led the 1950-51 Maple Leafs in playoff goals on their way to the Stanley Cup.

109

WINS BY A ROOKIE
[TERRY SAWCHUK, 44]

It seems like a no-brainer that in racking up 44 wins as a rookie, Terry Sawchuk would have won the Vezina Trophy in 1950-51. But fate and fine print conspired against the Red Wings netminder, who, historically, had to settle for the record of most victories in a season by a rookie.

Back then, the Vezina was awarded to the goaltender who played the majority of games for the team with the fewest goals against.

Sawchuk was in the running for the award, but on the last weekend of the season he was popped for three tallies by Montreal on the Saturday. On the Sunday, he shut out the Habs, but Toronto netminder Al Rollins – also an NHL freshman – blanked the Bruins after surrendering just one goal the night before. The Leafs ended up with 138 goals against on the season and Detroit 139, giving Rollins (27-5-8) the honor.

To further the injustice, the future Hall of Famer played all 70 games (44-13-13) for Detroit that season, while Rollins split time with veteran Turk Broda.

The Red Wings lost in a battle of goaltenders in the first round of the playoffs that year, too, as Montreal's Gerry McNeil (also a rookie) stymied the Detroit attack.

Sawchuk helped Detroit hoist the Stanley Cup three of the next four seasons and won the Vezina the same number of times in that span. Losing that initial trophy stung, particularly because the Maple Leafs were vocal in their dislike of the enigmatic netminder at the time, but Detroit brass did have one remedy to soften the blow. Back then, the Vezina came with a $1,000 bonus from the league. And even though Rollins got that prize, the Wings gave Sawchuk his own bonus for the same amount.

Though many great netminders have come along since, no one has been able to eclipse Sawchuk's mark of 44 freshman wins. Ed Belfour came closest, notching 43 with Chicago in 1990-91.

Terry Sawchuk was slotted at No. 1 in THN's 2011 rankings of the Top 100 Players of All-Time by Position.

110

YOUNGEST PLAYER
[ARMAND 'BEP' GUIDOLIN, 16]

An NHL rookie typically acts like a wide-eyed boy, just looking to keep his head down (off the ice, at least) as he wades through the trials and travails of his first season. But in one case, "boy" was a literal term.

Armand 'Bep' Guidolin set a record as the youngest NHLer ever when he began his career with Boston in 1942. Bep was 16 years, 11 months when he played his first game, a 3-1 loss to Toronto on Nov. 12.

At the time, the NHL was hit hard by players going off to serve in the Second World War. Numerous players were enlisting to fight in Europe and the Bruins were one of the worst-hit teams. Milt Schmidt, Woody Dumart and Bobby Bauer, the 'Kraut Line,' had finished 1-2-3 in league scoring in 1939-40. All three enlisted and were pressed into service before the 1942 playoffs began. They scored a combined 22 points their final game and were carried off the ice by players from *both* teams. The next season, a young whippersnapper named Bep began his career.

Guidolin didn't begin skating until he was 13, but scored 22 points as an NHL rookie three years later.

The left winger from Thorold, Ont., was a prodigy of sorts. He didn't begin skating until he was 13, but scored seven goals and 22 points in 42 games as an NHL rookie three years later. At 5-foot-8 and 175 pounds, Guidolin was of average size for the time and quickly became a better-than-average player, scoring 17 goals his second year at an age when teenagers today are in their draft year.

Barring a drastic change to the NHL's draft rules, Bep Guidolin's record for youngest player will never be broken.

In case you missed the point, because the NHL now has an 18-year-old draft, Guidolin holds a record that will never be broken.

When he was old enough – after his second NHL season – young Bep also enlisted. He spent the 1944-45 campaign in the military playing for navy and army teams based in and around Toronto before returning for another eight NHL seasons. He was allegedly run out of the league in 1952 for being an early advocate for a players union.

Guidolin played eight more seasons in various minor pro and senior leagues before hanging up his blades in 1961. Four seasons after retiring, Guidolin took up coaching. He began in the Ontario Hockey Association, forerunner to today's Ontario League, and by the early 1970s was back in the pro ranks.

When coaching the WHA's Edmonton Oilers, Guidolin got into a fight with Winnipeg Jets coach Bobby Kromm in 1976.

Guidolin's greatest coaching successes came during his return to where it all began with the Bruins. He took over for Tom Johnson with 26 games to play in 1972-73 and then led Bobby, Phil and the rest of the powerhouse Bruins back to the Stanley Cup final in 1974, losing to Philadelphia.

Andre Savard, who played 12 NHL seasons, from 1973 to 1985, before going on to management, coaching and scouting was, at 20 years of age, the youngest NHLer Guidolin ever coached.

"I can't say I got to know him very well," Savard said when asked if Guidolin had any advice from his days as a youngster in the NHL. "There wasn't as much communication as there is now."

Indeed, Guidolin, who died in November 2008, was old school. By the time he retired as a player, he was known as a guy who'd stand up for his teammates and was a penalty-minute leader in the old Quebec Senior League, a semi-pro loop best known for producing Jean Beliveau. His truculence continued in his days behind the bench. When coaching the World Hockey Association's Edmonton Oilers, Guidolin got into a fight with Winnipeg Jets coach Bobby Kromm in 1976. Players restrained the two after a shouting match between the benches ended with Guidolin landing the lone punch.

Savard remembers coach Guidolin being close to the Bruins veterans, not Boston's younger guys. And who can blame him.

"When you have Bobby Orr and Phil Esposito and Wayne Cashman and Ken Hodge and Johnny Bucyk, you've got a great, veteran team," Savard said. "Being a rookie on a veteran team, you just try to make your way."

You can bet that's how a 16-year-old Guidolin felt as the youngest NHLer in history. ∎ John Grigg

YOUNGEST PLAYER TO SCORE A HAT TRICK
[JORDAN STAAL, 18 YEARS, 153 DAYS]

111

Following in the footsteps of a prolific older brother in the hockey world has seldom led to similar results. For every Henri Richard there are 20 guys like Keith Gretzky, Brett Lindros and Steve Kariya.

As the second-born Staal in Thunder Bay's first family of hockey, Jordan Staal had to enter the league, as an 18-year-old rookie in 2006-07, trying to measure up to older brother Eric, a Stanley Cup champion the previous season.

Jordan quickly made a name for himself during his first campaign, playing an aggressive two-way game for the Pittsburgh Penguins.

On Feb. 17, 2007, Staal netted three goals – including the overtime winner – against Andrew Raycroft and the Toronto Maple Leafs to become the youngest player ever to record a hat trick, at 18 years, 153 days old. Prior to Staal, Leafs left winger Jack Hamilton – at 18 years, 185 days – held the record for more than 63 years.

Jordan Staal

That's a Stretch

Glenn Hall plays down his streak of consecutive games played, but the feat is remarkable by any standard.

CONSECUTIVE GAMES PLAYED BY A GOALIE
[GLENN HALL, 502]

112

Maybe he's being humble, maybe he's tired of the same question for half a century. Glenn Hall is just so matter-of-fact when it comes to talking about hockey's most untouchable record.

"You had to be lucky," Hall understated. "You had to stay healthy."

Make no mistake, Hall's record of 502 consecutive games between the pipes for Detroit and Chicago in the 1950s and '60s is an ironclad standard enveloped in kryptonite. Even Superman won't come close to touching this mark.

It's unusual for a skater to play that many consecutive games. For a goalie, it will never happen again. It would be a cover story in The Hockey News if any stopper made it to 10 percent of Hall's record.

"Playing in the NHL was the most important thing that happened to me. That was my highlight."

Glenn Hall

"Impossible," said noted hockey historian Ernie Fitzsimmons, from the Society of International Hockey Research. "With all the travel and the improved shooting skills by even the weakest players, and the goalie interference,...that makes it impossible to go every game."

Prior to NHL expansion in 1967, it was common for teams to rely on just one goalie. In more than a handful of cases, one goalie played the entire season without relief. But Hall did it for seven consecutive years until the morning of Nov. 7, 1962 when a pulled muscle in his back had him struggling to get out of bed.

"My back started bothering me a few days before," recalled Hall, a retired rancher living in Stony Plain, Alta. "I started a (Nov. 4) game and figured the adrenaline would carry me through as it had in the past. This time, it would not."

Chicago carried a 1-0 lead into the third period of that game against Detroit, but all was not right with Hall. He gave up three goals on seven shots and the Red Wings won 3-1. It was painful for Hall to bend over to untie his skates.

"I could throw up right now if you wanted."

Glenn Hall

The Hawks recalled Denis DeJordy in case Hall wasn't ready for the Nov. 7 game. The streak ended at 502 games and 49 years later that number is synonymous with the Hall of Fame stopper, even if it doesn't register with Hall.

"It's just a number," said Hall, now 79. "It doesn't mean that much. Just something that happened. Playing in the NHL was the most important thing that happened to me. That was my highlight."

At one point during Hall's run, he almost walked away from the streak and the game itself.

"The GM at the time (Chicago's Tommy Ivan) issued an edict that we would get a $100 fine for, what did he call it, indifferent play," Hall said. "I got it once for not playing to my full extent. The GM said, 'If you don't like the fine, quit.' So I contemplated that. I really, really did. I went back to my wife and we talked about it. The problem was I didn't know how to do anything else. The only thing I knew how to do is play goalie. So I paid the ransom and continued to play. That was the closest I came to stopping the streak."

There was another close call during the incredible run when Hall had a reaction to a penicillin shot. He said his eyes swelled up to the point he could barely see through two thin slits, but he played anyway.

Hall calls the streak "lucky," but perhaps it had something to do with his notorious pre-game ritual of vomiting prior to leaving the dressing room. It was his way of psyching himself up for a difficult task at hand. Hugging the porcelain just seemed to work.

"It was a case of playing well – I played well when I threw up before games," Hall said. "If I was just whistling relaxed, I was horseshit, so I forced myself and said this is everything, you've got to play well, you've got to play well."

So what was the ritual, Glenn? Spoon or fingers down your throat?

"No, no, no, you can do it mentally and I'd have a glass of water and go and do it," he said. "I could do it right now if you wanted."

Take a break, Glenn. You've earned it. ▌ Brian Costello

LONGEST SHUTOUT SEQUENCE [BRIAN BOUCHER, 332:01]

113

At one point in his career, Brian Boucher was supposed to be a No. 1 goaltender in the NHL. After all, he was the 22nd overall pick in the 1995 draft and, as a 23-year-old rookie, had a miniscule 1.91 GAA in 35 games with the Flyers.

Even after the Flyers decided to trade him to Phoenix, the plan in Arizona was that Boucher would become the team's No. 1 over time. But after one cringe-worthy season, he started the

For a five-game stretch in 2003-04, Brian Boucher left shooters howling for goals.

2003-04 campaign as the third-stringer behind Sean Burke and Zac Bierk.

It wasn't until Bierk sustained a hip injury that playing time became a reality for Boucher. He started slowly with a 5-1 loss to Tampa Bay and won only one of his first eight games. But Boucher got on track Dec. 31 with a 4-0 win at home against the Los Angeles Kings, which at first just seemed like a goalie snapping out of a slump as his team was heading out on a four-game road trip.

In reality, it was the start of a magical, record-setting run.

Travelling to Dallas, Carolina, Washington and Minnesota, Boucher didn't let a single puck past him at any stop along the way.

Travelling to Dallas, Carolina, Washington and, finally, Minnesota, Boucher didn't let a single puck past him at any stop along the way. In that final game against the Wild, Boucher knew how close he was to the 309:21 record Bill Durnan set 55 years earlier.

"I did look up at the clock," Boucher said at the time. "Once I saw it was, I think, four minutes into the third, I knew I could breathe easy as far as the streak is concerned."

With the streak intact, the Coyotes headed home to face the Atlanta Thrashers where Boucher finally had the crowd behind him. But at 6:16 of the first period an unlikely goal-scorer ended the shutout streak at 332:01 as Randy Robitaille's shot deflected in off Coyotes defenseman David Tanabe.

"It was kind of a cheesy goal to let in," Boucher said, who stopped 146 straight shots during the streak. "I kind of wish it had been a good goal – (Ilya) Kovalchuk beating me with a rocket top-shelf."

Boucher ended up playing 40 games for Phoenix that season and didn't post another clean sheet. Since moving on to other teams following the lockout, he's posted only five shutouts.

(Two goaltenders – Ottawa's Alec Connell, 461:29, in 1927-28 and Montreal's George Hainsworth, 343:05, in 1928-29 – did post longer streaks, but both were during the days before forward passing was allowed in all three zones.)

114 CONSECUTIVE GAMES WITH A GOAL [PUNCH BROADBENT, 16]

Not Joe Malone or Howie Morenz, not Wayne Gretzky or Brett Hull. None of the game's greatest goal-scorers can boast what Harry 'Punch' Broadbent can: a record 16 consecutive games with at least one goal.

It was the 1921-22 campaign and history was made on a number of fronts. The season went from two halves to one whole; goaltenders were allowed to pass the puck as far forward as their blueline; minor penalties were reduced from three minutes to two; the last pro game with seven players aside was contested; Sprague and Odie Cleghorn became the first brothers to score four goals for the same team in the same game; and the first tie game in NHL history was played.

In the middle of it all, Broadbent, an Ottawa Senator, produced one of the greatest individual efforts in league history. His record run began Christmas Eve, 1920 during a 10-0 rout of Montreal. Seven weeks later on Feb. 15, Broadbent scored in his 16th straight game, a 6-6 tie with the same Habs. His record bettered Malone's 14-game streak from four seasons earlier and will likely never be approached.

Broadbent, who died in 1971, was 29 at the time of the record. He was a fearless player whose 14-season career was interrupted for three years when he volunteered for duty in the First World War, earning the Military Medal for his distinguished service.

Broadbent earned the nickname 'Old Elbows' by his career's end.

At 5-foot-7 and 183 pounds, he was a stout right winger on one of the NHL's top scoring lines. But he was known as much for his two-way play and physical style as his scoring prowess. Broadbent is considered one of the game's original power forwards. He'd earned the nickname 'Old Elbows' by his career's end.

Broadbent won four Cups, three with Ottawa (1920, '21, '23) and one with the Montreal Maroons (1926) before retiring in 1929. He was inducted into the Hockey Hall of Fame in 1962.

CONSECUTIVE GAMES WITHOUT A LOSS BY A TEAM [PHILADELPHIA FLYERS, 35]

115

Thirty-five games. Three months. No losses.

The 1979-80 Flyers lost their second game of the season in early October and didn't lose again until Jan. 7. The undefeated record – 25-0-10 – still remains the standard for all North American professional teams.

One reason for the success? First, a good mixture of aging Hall of Famers (Bobby Clarke, Bill Barber), a wave of hungry new kids (Ken Linseman, Mel Bridgman, Behn Wilson) and a bunch of helpful plumbers (Frank Bathe, Norm Barnes, John Paddock, Mike Busniuk and Dennis Ververgaert) found its groove early.

Plus, rookie goaltender Pete Peeters and veteran Phil Myre were a perfect fit for each other.

"It was a great mix," Barber said. "We had a blend of the older and younger guys.

"The younger guys paid attention to listening and learning about what it took to win. We got great goaltending from Peeters. And when you're able to use your farm system and the minor leagues, that was an important factor for us that year. From Barnes to Bathe to Terry Murray, those players paid off for us."

"To not lose in 35 games, it was pretty special. I find it hard to believe that it will ever be done again."

Bill Barber

Coach Pat Quinn had his team playing the correct fashion. It would finish with a league-high 116 points (48-12-20) and take the New York Islanders to six games before falling in the Stanley Cup final.

"You talk about team play, playing the game the right way," Barber said, "there weren't any games that we were out of and not many teams can say that.

"To not lose in 35 games, it was pretty special. I find it hard to believe that it will ever be done again. That's almost half the season. We went to Atlanta in the second game of the season and got absolutely killed (9-2). From that point on we didn't lose until January." ∎ Wayne Fish

Bobby Clarke led the Flyers to an undefeated streak that tops not only hockey but all major sports in North America.

116

CONSECUTIVE SEASONS
OF 50 OR MORE GOALS
[MIKE BOSSY, 9]

Before there was Wayne Gretzky, Alex Ovechkin, Pavel Bure or Brett Hull, the biggest scoring threat in the NHL was a multi-skilled superstar who played for the New York Islanders in that franchise's heyday. His name was Mike Bossy.

Although he was a right winger adept at playmaking on the ice (of his 1,126 career points in just 752 games, 553 were assists), he made headlines for being one of the most consistent scoring threats in NHL history.

It was incredible when Bossy set the record for most goals as a rookie when he netted 53 in 1977-78 (later broken by Teemu Selanne), in the process becoming the first NHLer in history to score 50 or more in his freshman campaign. And it was outstanding when he set a league record with nine hat tricks in 1980-81 (later broken by Wayne Gretzky) and that same season broke Reggie Leach's record of 80 combined goals in a regular season and playoffs by amassing 85 for the Isles (68 and 17).

But above and beyond all those impressive achievements, the most spectacular was the fact Bossy was such a consistently dangerous offensive menace. He scored 50 or more goals for nine consecutive seasons, a feat no NHLer – not even the 'The Great One,' who managed only eight straight – has been able to match or better.

Given that injuries limited Bossy to just 10 seasons before retiring in 1987, the regularity with which he contributed offensively is a lasting source of pride for the sniper.

"Right from the start, being as consistent as I could be was my main focus and goal," said Bossy, who popped 50 from his rookie year to his penultimate season in 1985-86. "It's a record I'm extremely proud of, but it's one I couldn't have achieved without playing alongside great players and without being

In '80-81, Mike Bossy became the second player to pot 50 in 50 after 'Rocket' Richard first achieved the feat in '44-45. Only three players – Wayne Gretzky, Mario Lemieux and Brett Hull – have done so since.

lucky in the sense I didn't miss that many games during my career. Fifty was always a magic number for me."

Bossy's career high in goals during a single season was 69, set in his sophomore year, but no campaign was more memorable than 1980-81. That year, in addition to the aforementioned hat trick and combined goals records, Bossy scored 50 goals in 50 games, becoming only the second player to do so after Maurice Richard in 1944-45. Yet the perfectionist in Bossy believes he could have been even better that year.

"When I look back on it now, I didn't score that many goals in the last 32 games of the year," said Bossy, who had 18 markers in that span. "After the season was over, I admit to being a little disappointed I didn't get more than that."

> *"Right from the start, being as consistent as I could be was my main focus and goal."*
> Mike Bossy

Now 54 and a member of the Islanders organization once again, this time in a front office capacity, Bossy laments the chronic back problems that held him to only 63 games and 38 goals in his final season, believing he would have been in the unique position to be a 50-goal scorer for every year he played as an NHL professional. That confidence could be seen when he was asked whether any of his era's great goaltenders – Ken Dryden and Grant Fuhr among them – had his number and shook his confidence.

"I was never intimidated by any goalie," said Bossy, who won four Cups with the Isles and was awarded the Conn Smythe Trophy as MVP of the 1982 playoffs. "I just never let them intimidate me. I was always fairly confident in my abilities and always thought it was just a matter of numbers: the more shots I got on a goalie, the better opportunities I had and the more I was going to score. Letting the law of averages take over was the idea." ▌ Adam Proteau

CONSECUTIVE GAMES WITHOUT BEING SHUT OUT
[CALGARY FLAMES, 264 GAMES]

L ed by forwards Kent Nilsson, Guy Chouinard and Lanny McDonald and defenseman Paul Reinhart, the Calgary Flames boasted a solid offense in the early 1980s. And it was this core of players that would prevent the Flames from being shut out in the record 264 games between being blanked by the St. Louis Blues on Nov. 10, 1981, and the Quebec Nordiques on Jan. 11, 1985.

No team was able to completely close the door on the Flames.

During the streak, which spanned two complete seasons and more than half of two others, they were held to one goal on 20 occasions. But no team was able to completely close the door on them. Compare that to today when, since the lockout, only three teams have gone a full season without getting shut out and none approached two seasons.

The Los Angeles Kings threatened the record a few years after it was set, but the Flames held them scoreless on Oct. 25, 1989, just two games shy of tying the record.

Red Light District

GOALS SCORED IN ONE PLAYOFF SERIES
[EDMONTON OILERS, 44]

The Edmonton Oilers philosophy was quite simple, really: Score, score, score. No matter how many goals the other guys get, just get more.

It served them well.

After eliminating the Los Angeles Kings and Winnipeg Jets from the playoffs during the 1984-85 season, the red-hot Oilers' next challenge was the Chicago Black Hawks. Having beaten Chicago in all three regular season meetings by a combined score of 17-9, the Oilers were primed to roll over the Hawks.

But even the most ardent Edmonton supporter had to be a bit surprised when the Oilers won the first game by an staggering 11-2 count. And to prove that was no fluke, the Oilers whipped the Black Hawks 7-3 in Game 2. Although Chicago won Games 3 and 4 at home by scores of 5-2 and 8-6, the Oilers closed the series and advanced to the Stanley Cup final with wins of 10-5 and 8-2.

> *"People ask me how Wayne could get 215 points in one season and I always tell them it's because he was trying for 300."*
>
> Paul Coffey

In total, the Oilers scored an NHL record 44 goals in that series. What would the record be if the Black Hawks had somehow managed to stretch it to seven games? We'll never know, but if Edmonton stayed true to the rate they scored at in the series (7.3 per game), the Oilers would have tallied 51 goals had the series gone the limit. As it is, the record is plenty safe. Even the Oilers themselves couldn't come close to their one-series output again: the 1983 squad is tied with the 1995 Calgary Flames for second place with 35.

Wayne Gretzky was the catalyst on an Edmonton Oilers squad that rewrote the record book on a mind-boggling number of fronts.

Superstar defenseman Paul Coffey said the high-flying Oilers were a reflection of their leader, Wayne Gretzky.

"If we scored two goals, we wanted to get three," Coffey said. "We were a little bit like the (Los Angeles) Lakers in that we pushed the pace all the time. People ask me how Wayne could get 215 points in one season and I always tell them it's because he was trying for 300. That's what people pay to see – goals. Wayne was funny; if he got a goal early it just motivated him to push for more."

Added fellow defenseman Kevin Lowe, one of the few Oilers who actually gave a hoot about preventing goals: "Think of a team that is young and just coming into its own. We had won the Stanley Cup the year before and we were convinced we had the talent to do it again. The truth of the matter is, the Black Hawks really didn't stand a chance against us."

"The truth of the matter is, the Black Hawks really didn't stand a chance against us."
Kevin Lowe

Not surprisingly, Gretzky, who won the Hart Trophy as the NHL's most valuable player in the regular season and the Conn Smythe Trophy for being playoff MVP, led Edmonton against Chicago with four goals and 18 points in the series. He led the playoffs in scoring with 17 goals and 47 points in 18 games. Jari Kurri, who was riding shotgun on a line with 'The Great One,' managed 12 goals and 15 points against Chicago, while speedy winger Glenn Anderson and Coffey each had 14 points.

Only four Edmonton skaters – role players Billy Carroll, Don Jackson, Dave Lumley and Dave Semenko – failed to register a point in the series.

Chicago goalie Murray Bannerman finished the playoffs with a respectable 9-6 record, but his post-season goals-against average, 4.77, was thanks largely to the Oilers. Bannerman, who appeared in two NHL All-Star Games, was lit up like a department store Christmas tree. The Oilers were No. 1 in goals-for in the regular season with 401 and they continued to play the same firewagon hockey in the playoffs.

The Oilers actually got a bit of a scare in the opening game of the Stanley Cup final, losing by a score of 4-1. However, they rallied to win the series in five games, outscoring Philadelphia 21-14 in total.

Even though most remember Edmonton as being a team that bucked the notion of team defense, Lowe insists that was not the case.

"(Coach) Glen Sather actually stressed that we play a defensive system," Lowe said. "By that, I mean we were free to score as many goals as we could, but we were expected to come back and help in our own zone. The thing is we had the best players and we were hard to stop. We had the confidence to win and we had the best talent." ∎ Mike Brophy

GOALS BY A TEAM IN ONE GAME [MONTREAL CANADIENS, 16]

119

The Quebec Bulldogs lasted one season in the NHL, but were around long enough to find themselves on the wrong side of the history books when they were blasted by the Montreal Canadiens 16-3 on March 3, 1920.

Nineteen-year-old Bulldogs goaltender Frank Brophy was exploited for all 16 tallies during what would be his only season in the NHL. He gave up four goals in the first period, seven in the second and five in the third.

Amos Arbour finished the game with two goals, but his solid night was buried on this day as four players recorded hat tricks. Player/coach Edward 'Newsy' Lalonde and defenseman Harry Cameron each had four goals while right wingers Didier Pitre and Odie Cleghorn had three apiece. The four hat tricks in one game is also an NHL record.

FASTEST TWO GOALS BY BOTH TEAMS
[ST. LOUIS BLUES VS. BOSTON BRUINS, 2 SECONDS]

Down 6-4 to the Blues on Dec. 19, 1987, Ken Linseman scored at 19:50 of the third period to bring the Bruins within one. Dreams of a miracle comeback were dashed in the blink of an eye, however, when Blues center Doug Gilmour answered two seconds later by scoring into an empty net off the ensuing faceoff.

Doug Smail didn't need the assistance of a man advantage to pop 31 goals in 1984-85.

GOALS WITHOUT A POWER PLAY GOAL IN ONE SEASON
[DOUG SMAIL, 31]

I n a 13-year NHL career otherwise marked with consistency and third-line checking prowess, Doug Smail had a number of unusual distinctions.

He set the record for the fastest goal to open a game, when he scored five seconds into a Dec. 20, 1981 match between his Winnipeg Jets and St. Louis. (That record has since been tied by Bryan Trottier in 1984 and Alexander Mogilny in 1991.)

Smail also holds the Winnipeg/Phoenix mark for career shorthanded goals with 25. He'll hold that for a good, long time, too. Shane Doan is the active leader with six.

Smail is also the first player to go directly from the NHL to a British team when he left the Ottawa Senators in 1992-93 at 35 to sign with the Fife Flyers the next season.

It wasn't from a lack of effort - it was from a lack of opportunity.

But Smail's often-overlooked distinction is holding the record for scoring the most goals in a season without one of them being a power play tally. All 31 of Smail's tallies for the Jets in 1984-85 were at even strength or shorthanded. But it wasn't from a lack of effort – it was from a lack of opportunity. The Jets had five other 30-goal scorers on that team and they – Dale Hawerchuk, Paul MacLean, Thomas Steen, Laurie Boschman and Brian Mullen – along with Perry Turnbull were all on the first and second power play units.

A native of Moose Jaw, Sask., who spent three years at the University of North Dakota, Smail found his niche in a checking-line capacity. In all but one of his first seven full seasons, Smail had point totals in the 31-to-49 range. But during that one magical season, he had 31 goals and 66 points playing with the grinding likes of Scott Arniel, Ron Wilson and Jim Nill.

"His speed created most of his opportunities," Nill said. "He didn't receive quality time on the power play. He was very good on the PK – he could have had more goals with the chances he created."

"It's an amazing record people don't know about."

Jim Nill

Only 27 players in 2010-11 scored 31 or more goals. The highest scorer without a PPG was Lauri Korpikoski with 19. In 2009-10, it was Patrice Bergeron, again with 19. Alex Burrows came close to the record in 2008-09 with 28 markers.

"It's an amazing record people don't know about," Nill said. "It's not something we ever discussed in the dressing room and I don't remember the media ever picking up on it." ❚ Brian Costello

122

GAME-WINNING GOALS IN ONE PLAYOFF SERIES
[MIKE BOSSY, 4]

Scoring a game-winning goal at the highest level of the sport is something every hockey fan dreams of. Only a fraction of one percent of those people realize that dream – and only one player in the history of the NHL has ever scored all four winners in the same playoff series.

That's what New York Islanders legend Mike Bossy did during the 1983 Wales Conference final against Boston.

Although he was famous for many reasons (including scoring two Cup-winning goals during the four consecutive Islander titles), one of the right winger's biggest achievements was putting up one of the greatest individual efforts the game has seen: a team-best nine goals and 13 points in the six-game series against a Bruins team that had the NHL's best record.

"I haven't forgotten that great series," Bossy said. "That was memorable."

"Winning was all that mattered, but it was fun to contribute like that."
Mike Bossy

After picking up the winning goal in each of three Isles victories, Bossy saved his best for the finale. In Game 6, Bossy had a four-goal night in New York's 8-4 win over Boston.

That was the exclamation point for his answer to starting that post-season slowly – at least, for him – with six goals in 10 games against the Isles first- and second-round opponents.

"I had a lot of chances that weren't going in earlier in the playoffs, so it felt like the odds were starting to even out for me against Boston," Bossy said. "Winning was all that mattered, but it was fun to contribute like that."

Bossy's contribution is a record that can never be broken… barring the unlikely introduction of the best-of-nine playoff format. ▌ Adam Proteau

GOAL DEFICIT OVERCOME IN ONE PLAYOFF GAME
[LOS ANGELES KINGS, 5]

The 1981-82 Edmonton Oilers were a team on the verge of greatness. Boasting the second best record in the NHL that season, the Oilers captured the Smythe division by an astounding 34 points over their closest competitor, scored an NHL record 417 goals and boasted a plethora of future stars named Messier, Coffey, Kurri, Anderson and Fuhr. Each of them, however, toiled in the shadow of Wayne Gretzky. In 1981-82 he had rewritten the record book posting 92 goals, 120 assists and 212 points – each of them a new NHL standard.

Edmonton's opposition in their first-round best-of-five playoff series was the lowly Los Angeles Kings. Of the 16 playoff qualifiers the Kings possessed the worst record (a full 48 points behind the Oilers), allowed the most goals and scored the fourth fewest.

> *"There was bedlam in the building."*
> Bob Miller

The Oilers-Kings matchup appeared to be a gross mismatch. The desperate Kings, advocating a strategy that was designed to see them outscore the Oilers rather than attempt to shut them down, did just that in the first game, coming away with a shocking 10-8 win. The combined 18 goals are still an NHL record for most in a playoff game.

Game 2 saw the Oilers bounce back with a 3-2 overtime win. The series switched to L.A. for the third game, where the enthusiasm of the home crowd was quickly extinguished by Edmonton, which jumped out to a seemingly insurmountable 5-0 lead.

Daryl Evans scored the OT
game-winner in the most
memorable game in Kings
history.

For Bob Miller, the Kings play-by-play man since 1973 there was a sense of another opportunity squandered: "There was so much anticipation before the game. The Kings always had struggled to gain a foothold in Los Angeles and we now had everybody excited and then we go in the dumper."

Miller wasn't alone in his disgust. Below him the crowd noticeably thinned as many made their way to the exits, including Kings owner Jerry Buss.

"You were hoping that they could at least break the shutout," remembered Miller.

The Kings did break the shutout with two quick goals at the start of the third. But it was the their third tally with a little more than five minutes left that marked a turning point.

"The crowd was beginning to realize that there was a chance," Miller said. "That's when the atmosphere in the building changed and the momentum started to build."

"I'll never forget Grant Fuhr. You could almost see the pained expression on his face, even with the mask on."

Bob Miller

The fourth goal soon followed and in Miller's words "there was bedlam in the building." The pandemonium extended to the parking lot where those who had left prematurely closely listened on the radio and had begun their own celebration.

But the score still remained 5-4 Edmonton. And as the clock clicked down it seemed the Oilers would survive. With 10 seconds remaining the puck comfortably rested on the stick of Wayne Gretzky. All he had to do was clear it from his own end and the game would end. Yet for one brief, rare moment Gretzky's soft hands betrayed him and coughed up the disc. Before anybody could react the puck was in the back of the Oilers net. With five seconds left in the game the score was deadlocked at fives.

"The Forum was in an uproar," Miller remembered, the excitement in his voice still palpable almost three decades later. "There was a break before overtime to flood the ice, but the people never stopped chanting, they walked around pumping their fists in the air...the building was electric."

No team in playoff history had ever come back from a 5-0 deficit. The impossible seemed inevitable and the Kings' Daryl Evans ended the game at the 2:35 mark of overtime with a one-timer over Grant Fuhr's glove. Flailing his arms in the air, an exuberant Evans raced to the other side of the rink.

The Oilers stood in shock.

"I'll never forget Grant Fuhr," Miller said. "You could almost see the pained expression on his face, even with the mask on."

Forgotten in time is the fact the Oilers won Game 4 before losing at home 7-4 in the series-concluding game. In retrospect, the loss to the Kings was a catalyst for the Oilers, who never again took an opponent so lightly. During the next eight years, Edmonton appeared in six Stanley Cup finals, winning five times.

The Kings quickly fell in the next round, but the memories of the Miracle on Manchester lingered. In addition to the record for most goals in a game, set in the opening contest, the largest playoff comeback in Game 3 and the largest upset (48-point difference) in NHL playoff history over the course of the series, the two teams combined for 50 goals, an NHL record for a five-game series. The Kings set a record with 27 goals in a five-game series.

Five unforgettable games, five NHL records and a Miracle.

"There isn't a day that goes by where someone doesn't stop me to tell me that they were at the Forum that night for the Miracle on Manchester," Miller said. "Even thinking about it today I still get goosebumps." ∎ Todd Denault

SHORTHANDED GOALS BY A TEAM IN ONE SEASON
[EDMONTON OILERS, 36]

t was considered a monumental achievement, a freak occurrence, when the Boston Bruins shattered the record for shorthanded goals in one season with 25 in 1970-71. The 1964-65 Chicago Black Hawks held the previous record of 14 and the Bruins dynamited that by 79 percent.

Boston shutdown specialist Ed Westfall led the Bruins with seven shorthanded goals, while third-liners Don Marcotte and Derek Sanderson each had six. It was a record pundits said would last forever.

Then the Edmonton Oilers came around and completely changed the conventional thinking that the best way to kill penalties is to put your defensive forwards on the ice. The talented Oilers of the 1980s viewed shorthanded situations as an opportunity for offensive stealth attacks.

The Oilers blitzed opposing power plays with 36 markers while a man short, obliterating Boston's record by 44 percent.

Led by Wayne Gretzky's record 12 shorthanded goals, the 1983-84 Oilers blitzed opposing power plays with 36 markers while a man short, obliterating Boston's record by 44 percent. Jari Kurri had five shorthanded goals, while Mark Messier and Glenn Anderson had four apiece.

The trick was to counterattack when the opposition had a clear manpower advantage. It worked like a charm. The four highest totals of shorthanded goals in one season are all held by Oilers teams of the 1980s. The 36 in '83-84, 28 in '86-87, and 27 in '85-86 and '88-89.

What's remarkable is the New Jersey Devils scored a league-low 51 power play goals that '83-84 season, a total not too much higher than Edmonton's 36 shorthanded tallies.

To further appreciate Edmonton's unique and skilled approach, note that just one team in the NHL in 2009-10 had a double-digit total in SHG – Chicago with 13.

The Oilers did a lot more than score while a man down that season. They set a record with 446 goals, an average of 5.58 per game. That's more than the game average for *both* teams in all the seasons of the Dead Puck Era.

WINS BY A TEAM IN ONE SEASON
[DETROIT RED WINGS, 62]

125

For the past quarter century or so, the Detroit Red Wings have represented the best the NHL has to offer, finishing first in their division 16 times and winning four Stanley Cups.

But even by their lofty standards, the Red Wings' 1995-96 season was one of extreme dominance. Detroit was far and away the best team in the NHL that year, winning the President's Trophy for the second time (the award was founded in 1985-86) – and by a margin of victory no other team before or since has matched or bettered.

In the then-26-team league, the Wings won a whopping 62 games, lost only 13 and tied seven for 131 points in the standings. The next closest franchise was the Colorado Avalanche, who finished with 15 fewer victories, a 47-25-10 record and 27 fewer points. Detroit lost just three games at home and only 10 on the road.

Chris Osgood, Mike Vernon, Scotty Bowman and Sergei Fedorov took home hardware from the 1996 NHL Awards.

Their brilliance could be seen in all areas: only Mario Lemieux's Pittsburgh Penguins had more goals-for (362 to 325) and no team allowed fewer goals than the 181 Detroit surrendered. Incredibly, their goals for/against differential of plus-144 was 58 better than that of the second-place Avs.

> ## *"That was a year just about everything went right for the organization."*
> ### Jim Devellano

The Scotty Bowman-coached Wings couldn't parlay the outstanding regular season into ultimate playoff success, however, falling to the Avs in six games in the Western Conference final. But through the first 82 games, nobody could touch them.

"That was a year just about everything went right for the organization," said long-time Red Wings executive Jim Devellano, who was the team's GM in 1995-96. "We had Sergei Fedorov and Steve Yzerman in their prime, Nicklas Lidstrom just entering his best years and a fantastic tandem in net of Mike Vernon and Chris Osgood. The playoffs turned out to be another story, but that regular season was us finding out just how good we could be." ∎ Adam Proteau

ACKNOWLEDGEMENTS

Publishing *Hockey's Most Amazing Records* required an effort for the ages from everyone involved and we're thankful for the hard work of the first-line stars to the black aces (you know who you are). Special thanks to:

The Hockey News editor in chief, Jason Kay, for keeping the team in line and motivated throughout. Edward Fraser, the magazine's managing editor, for directing traffic and ensuring all aspects received the treatment they deserved. Ronnie Shuker for his patience and dedication in proofreading. And Marie-Suzanne Menier for ensuring all the final details were taken care of.

The THN staff – Rory Boylen, Ken Campbell, Ryan Dixon, John Grigg, Ryan Kennedy, Adam Proteau – and the interns – Jordan Allard, Michael Amato, Jeff Blay, Patrick Cwiklinski, Marc Girard, Christine Gosselin, Remy Greer, Tim Kolupanowich, Chris Lund – for their tireless writing, editing and fact-checking.

Freelancers Mike Brophy, Todd Denault, Bob Duff, Eric Duhatschek, Wayne Fish, Jim Gintonio, Jay Greenberg, Mackenzie Liddell, Mike Loftus, John Vogl, Brian McNally, Jeremy Rutherford, Michael Russo and Eric Zweig for their expertise and creativity.

The players, coaches, GMs, personalities and media-types for taking the time to share their memories.

The art team of Jamie Hodgson (cover design), Erika Vanderveer (photo research), Diane Marquette (layout), Annick Désormeaux (page design) and Anne-Laure Jean (page design).

The management team of THN publisher Caroline Andrews and book publisher Jean Paré for their work behind the scenes.

And to the members of the marketing/communications department, Janis Davidson-Pressick, Carlie McGhee and Alyson Young for helping to get the word out.

PHOTO CREDITS